SONIA DELAUNAY
Fashion and Fabrics

SONIA

JACQUES DAMASE

With 180 illustrations, 104 in color

DELAUNAY
Fashion and Fabrics

THAMES
AND
HUDSON

Translations from the French by
Shaun Whiteside and Stanley Baron

Special photography by André Morain

Published in paperback in the
United States of America in 1997 by
Thames and Hudson Inc., 500 Fifth Avenue,
New York, New York 10110

Library of Congress Catalog
Card Number 96-61494
ISBN 0-500-27947-0

Printed and bound in Singapore

Contents

SONIA Delaunay's perenniality has been demonstrated for more than sixty years. As early as 1913 (she was born in Russia in 1885) she invented pasted cutouts, a technique which Matisse was to use towards the end of his life; in that period she influenced Paul Klee; forty years before the American painters she was playing with stripes; in 1925 she was designing clothes which could be worn today without appearing old-fashioned; she foresaw the future trends in fashion and interior decoration; beginning in 1912, she overturned the laws or rules of painting. Even today, she belongs to the avant-garde and remains no less astonishing a phenomenon than she was in 1925, when Robert Delaunay wrote of her: 'She carries within herself that warmth, that characteristic oriental mysticalness which, far from being destroyed by contact with the West, is reborn and finds its constructive expression in this contact, grows and develops a transformation in which the elements that constitute her art are transfused into a new art, comprising both eastern and western characteristics – formal and indivisible, so to speak – of which she alone has created the mould.'

To begin with, Sonia Delaunay's art was one of the first expressions of abstract painting, and one that proved to be most fruitful. It should not be forgotten that Sonia rallied to abstract art as early as 1912: her illustration for La Prose du Transsibérien, by her friend Blaise Cendrars, is without any doubt the first application of abstraction in decorative art, and her 'simultaneous contrasts' are among the earliest examples of that aesthetic.

But if it is not unimportant for the historian that her works preceded those of Malevich or Mondrian, from the art-lover's point of view it is more significant that they offered abstract painting a formula of which, regretfully, it did not take advantage. As distant from Kandinsky's theoretical canvases

Sonia Delaunay in a tunic of *rabanne* (embroidered straw), Madrid 1918

as from Kupka's, many 'inobjective' paintings (as Sonia Delaunay herself called them) which she made between 1912 and 1914 unite the rigour of simple geometric forms with an inner life and poetry which emanate from the richness of the colour, the musicality of the rhythm, the vibrant breadth of the execution. By bringing order and lyricism together, she proposes a synthesis which abstract painters rejected much to their loss, preferring on the one hand an intellectual, voluntaristic geometricism, or on the other an expressionism in which the fruitful complexity of 'electric prisms' was fragmented and impoverished.

It is time (Sonia Delaunay would have been 100 years old in 1985) to recognize in her the most permanent artist of the twentieth century. Polychrome architect, painter of the inner life and poet, poet nourished by immunity, by humanity, stripped of all literature ... Let us admire this lesson in freedom and life which she offers to all who have the eyes and the heart to perceive rhythms and colours.

Jacques Damase

Dress, drawing in Indian ink, 1925

7

Simultaneous Dress

For Mme Delaunay

On the dress she has a body.
The woman's body has as many bumps as my skull
Glorious if you are incarnate
With Wit
The tailors do a stupid job
Just like phrenology
My eyes are kilos weighing down the sensuality of women.
Everything that bumps progresses into depth
The stars penetrate the sky.
The colours disrobe in contrast.
'On the dress she has a body'.

Beneath the heather's arms
Shade halfmoons and pistils
When the water flows into the back with its blue-green shoulder-blades
And the double conch of the breasts passing beneath
        the bridge of rainbows
Belly
Discs
Sun
And the perpendicular cries of the colours fall on to the thighs
Saint Michael's sword
There are hands stretching out
In the train there is the beast, all the eyes, all the fanfares,
        all the customs of the Bal Bullier
And on the hip
The signature of the poet.

Blaise Cendrars 1914

**Sonia Delaunay in a 'simultaneous dress'
for the Bal Bullier, 1913**

1 **Patchwork quilt, 1911**

2 **Bookbinding, collage of fabrics, 1913**

3 **Carpet design, 1925** (opposite)

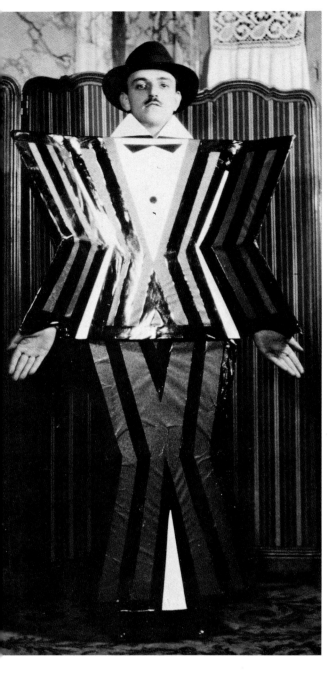

4,6 **Fancy dress costume designs, 1923**

5 **Printed silk** (variant on next page)

7,8 **Printed silks, c. 1926**

9 **SD dresses modelled against an**
  automobile painted by the artist, 1925

10 **Printed silk, 1926**

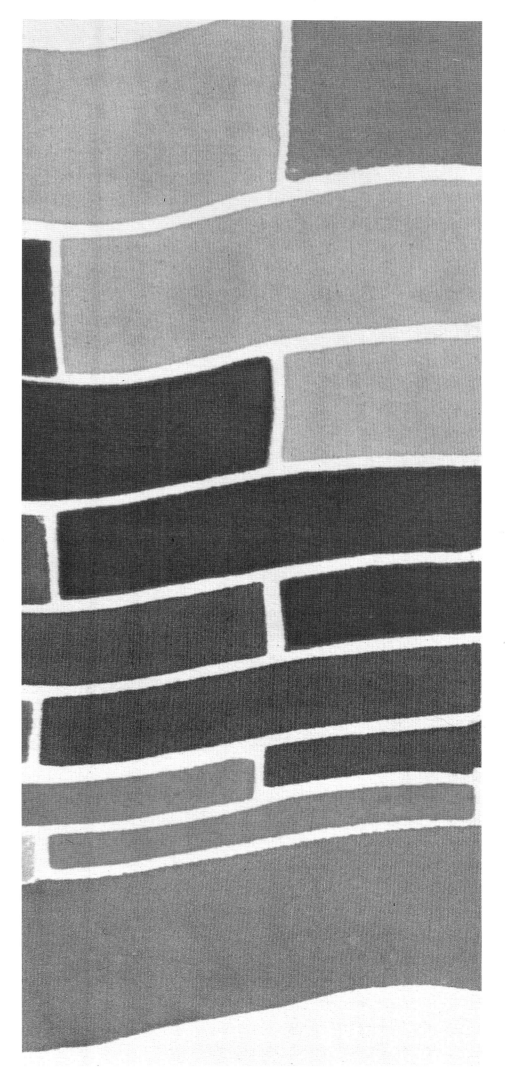

11 **Fashion design, 1924**

12 **Carpet design, 1928**

13 **Fabric design, 1924**

14 **Cover of an album, 1925**

15 **Sportwear design, 1925**

16 **Printed silk, 1925**

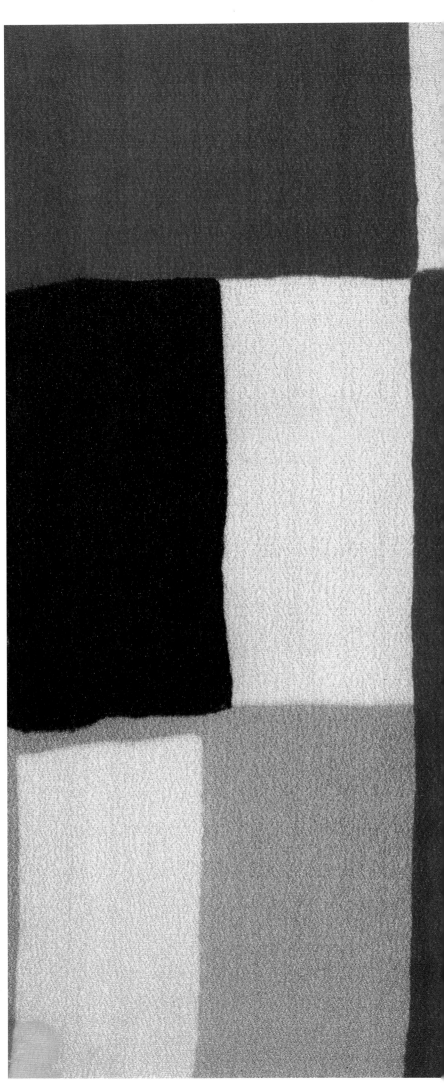

17,18 **Fabric designs, 1923**

20 **Printed silk furnishing fabric**

21 **René Crevel wearing a waistcoat
designed by SD, 1923/24**

22 **Dressing gown made of a fabric
designed by SD, 1926**

23,24 **Two silk fabrics, c. 1927**

25 **Printed linen, c. 1926**
(p. 32)

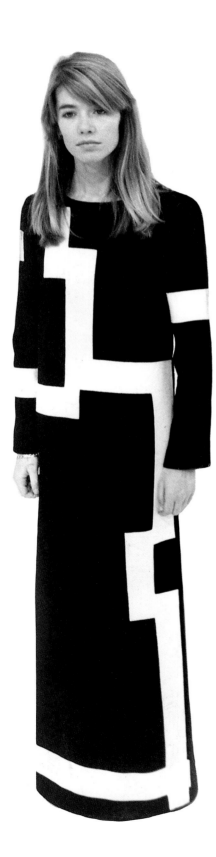

26 **Françoise Hardy wearing a copy of a dress designed by SD in 1925**

27 **Printed linen**

28,29 **Printed silks,
c. 1927**

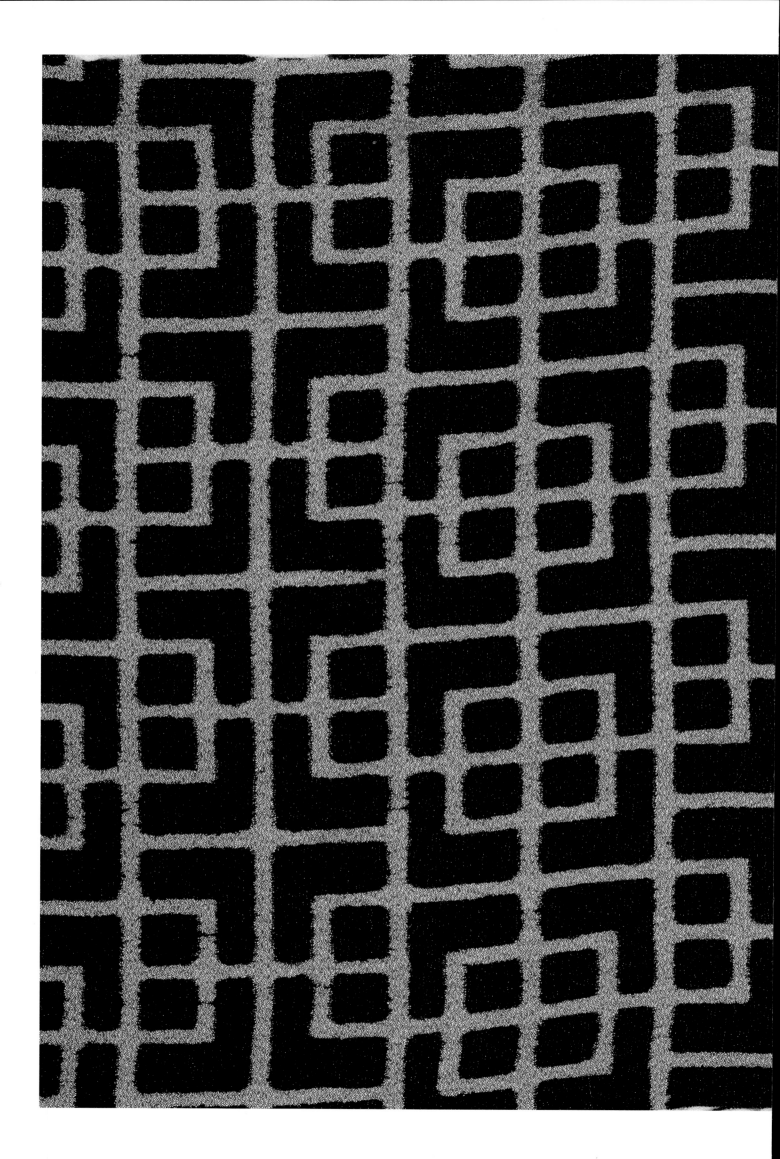

31 **Evening gown, c. 1924**

32 **Printed silk, 1922/23**

30 **Crêpe de chine silk designed for Chanel around 1928** (previous page)

33,34 **Two gouache designs on paper, c. 1935**

35,36 **Two fabric designs, 1928**

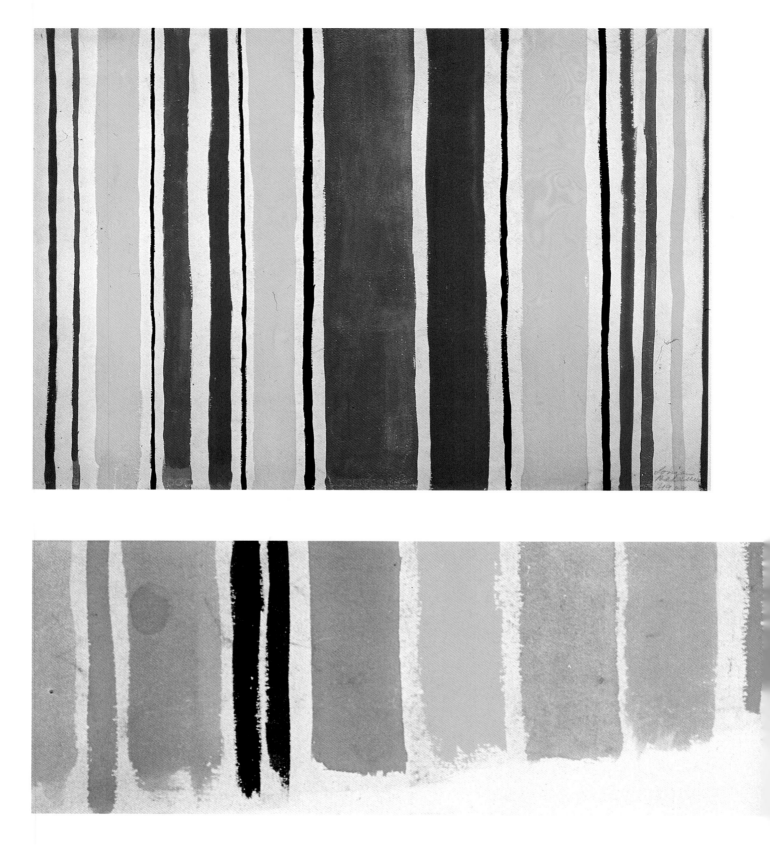

37,38 **Striped fabric designs, 1928**

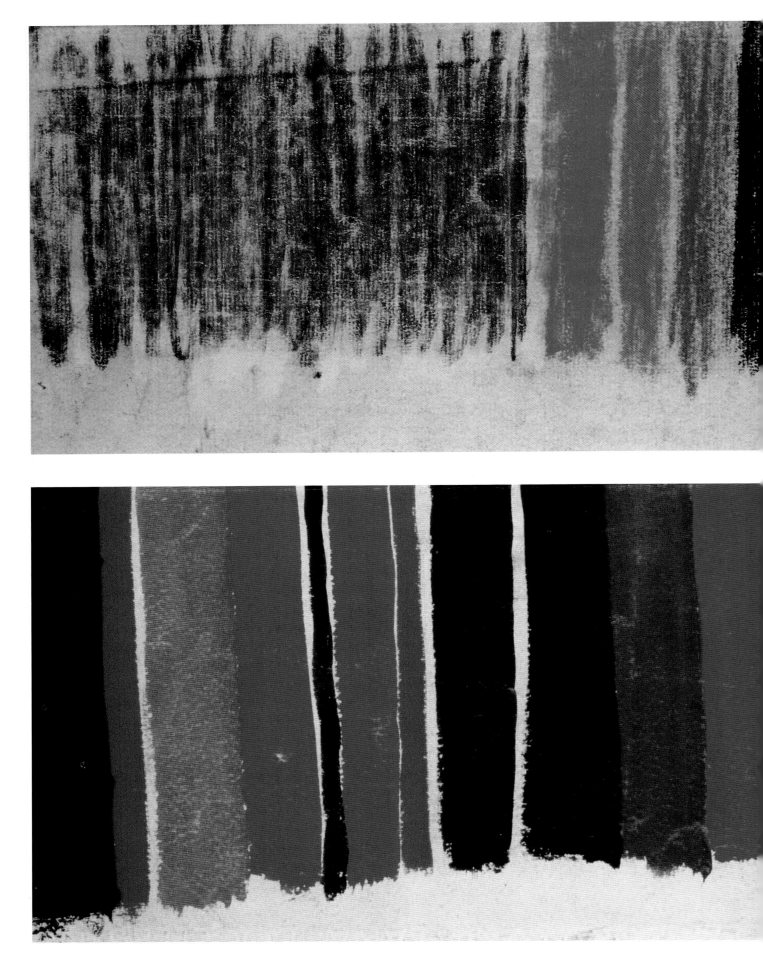

39,40 **Colour scale for striped fabrics, 1928**

42 **Fabric design, 1926**

43 **SD showing off one of
her fabrics, c. 1926**

44,45 **SD around 1930, wearing a fabric similar to the one shown**

IN 1923 a firm in Lyons ordered some fabric designs from Sonia. 'I have done fifty designs,' she said, 'relationships of colour using pure geometrical forms with rhythm. As far as I'm concerned, they were and remain colour scales – really a purified version of our concept of painting. It has involved a great deal of research and study. The research was purely pictorial, a plastic discovery which has served Delaunay as well as me in our painting. The rhythm is based on numbers, for colour can be measured by the number of vibrations. This is a completely new concept, one which opens infinite horizons for painting and may be used by everyone who can feel and understand it.'

Daniel Abadie wrote, 'Even if everybody agrees to recognize that the colours she applied to women's dresses, automobiles, posters have given streets their modern look, it is less well known that, consciously or not, contemporary painting owes a number of its discoveries to her.' But it was encouraging to see recognition, in an exhibition as important as the 'Paris-New York' show mounted at the Centre Pompidou in 1977, that Sonia had an influence on certain American painters in 1912–13 and that Jasper Johns and other well-known painters sometimes seem coincidentally to take up again Sonia's ideas of around 1925 – for example, the use of stripes. In 1927, she gave a lecture on 'The Influence of Painting on the Art of Clothes' to a conference at the Sorbonne organized by 'the group of philosophical and scientific studies'. She was always captivated by any movement which sought to fuse creativity with production. The following are some excerpts from her talk (note that the 'fabric pattern' which she mentions inaugurates the reign of ready-to-wear):

'. . . at the present time, fashion is passing through a critical stage which corresponds to a period of revolution. Some time before the First World War

46 **SD surrounded by some of her fabric designs, 1965**

Black snake, scarf created in 1924

it began to free itself from academic couture: it got rid of the corset, the high collar, all those elements of women's dress demanded by the aesthetic of fashion but which were contrary to hygiene and freedom of movement.

'It is mainly the change in women's lives that has provoked this revolution. Women are increasingly active . . .

'After the destructive period — the liberation from academic shackles — fashion, as it is now, clearly influenced by painting, must become constructive.

'Construction, the cut of a dress, is to be conceived at the same time as its decoration.

'This new concept leads us logically to an invention recently patented by Robert Delaunay, and first executed by me in collaboration with the House of Redfern. This is the fabric pattern. The cut of the dress is conceived by its creator simultaneously with its decoration. Then the cut and the decoration suitable to the shape are both printed on the same fabric.

'Hence the first collaboration of the creator of the model with the creator of the fabric. This is from the point of view of the artistic conception. From the point of view of the standardization which affects all modern trends, the fabric pattern makes it possible to reproduce the garment at the other end of the world for the least cost and a minimal waste of fabric. Thus when selling a length of cloth, one will be selling the cut and the decoration simultaneously.

'Those who consider the present movement transitory are mistaken. They may try to announce each new season that geometric designs will soon disappear from fashion to be replaced by new borrowings from old patterns, but they are making a grave mistake: geometric designs will never go out of fashion because they have never been *in* fashion . . .

'If we use geometric forms, it is because these simple and manageable elements seem suitable to the distribution of colour; and it is the relationships between colours that make up the real object of our studies. But these geometric forms do not form the essence of our art; the distribution of colours can be applied just as well to more complex forms, such as flowers — it simply calls for a somewhat more delicate handling.

Idea for an 'alternative rhythms' fabric, drawing in Indian ink, c. 1925

'A movement is now influencing fashion, just as it influences interior decoration, the cinema, and all the visual arts, and it overtakes everything that is not subject to this new principle which painters have spent a century seeking; we are only at the beginning of the study of these new colour relationships, still full of mysteries to unravel, which are at the base of a modern vision. We may be able to enrich them, complete them, develop them – even others than us will be able to continue our work – but there is no going back to the past . . .'

The most striking and, to me, the most important thing is Sonia Delaunay's durability; having overflown, surmounted, every fashion of this century, she is still there, and even today her works of sixty years ago proclaim the future, the year 2000.

This surprising, fantastic and most exceptional accomplishment has been equalled only by certain Bauhaus architects, such as Marcel Breuer, Walter Gropius, Mies van der Rohe, who invented in the '20s or earlier a few houses, a few pieces of furniture, a few chairs which seem imperishable and which will never go out of style. For example, the fabrics created by Sonia Delaunay between 1922 and 1930 can disappoint fans of 1920s style, or of nostalgia. They have been copied and recopied, but some of them retain a freshness, a newness and a classicism which astonish even their admirers.

Where does this permanence, this durability come from? Is it through the use of a new 'golden section'? Or an innate sense of rhythm, which is life itself? Or that incomparable freshness that led some of her friends to call her 'that eternally young Russian girl'. The magic of the hand that shuns all rules. Liberty in the grandest sense of that word, structure and architecture which are not apparent at first glance, but which are omnipresent. A fabulous and mathematical logic, linking up, overlapping of the seemingly simplest forms. Miracles and talent can no more be analyzed than the reasons for lucidity. An apparently reduced vocabulary, frank colours, a rigorous discipline do not take away that thrill from the work, a palpitation derived from pure sensibility, the most constructed lyricism in which colour and forms engender

and fulfill one another in the act which is movement. Dynamism gives the work its tension. Works in which the artist, with supreme freedom, distributes the liveliest contrasts within the order of an architectural style.

Her rectangles, triangles, squares, curves, enchant us with the mystery of a dynamism which is hers alone. From these elements, in principle straight and cold, Sonia Delaunay succeeds in creating a warm and sunny work such as life itself should be.

Mysterious and secret, this painting, these fabrics, help us to live. Rational in the irrational, Sonia establishes trajectories of sensibility linked to pure colour. Of this psycho-physiological vision, the art of the future — I repeat — we were given a premonition many dozens of years in advance.

Pierre Francastel wrote, 'With the Delaunays, the figuration of the qualitative values of movement: direction, speed, play of colours, observed at the instant of any motion, enters into the elementary material of contemporary art.' Was the discovery of simultaneism the essence of this youth?

Jacques Damase

DANSE DE LA ROBE
SONIA DELAUNAY-T
1922.

ROBERT Delaunay and his wife, Sonia Delaunay, were the first to attempt to purify the art of their time. Starting from the principle that in order to attain completeness a painting must have not only the qualities of material, design and colour but also a certain decorative sense – a certain geometrical simplicity of contour – they began a series of experiments related to economy in paintings, furniture and clothing.

Using her works on canvas in her quest to achieve the sharpest of colour contrasts – according to the laws of the ancients which had been forgotten for two centuries, partly rediscovered by Delacroix and codified by the brilliant Seurat, the theorist of *simultaneous contrast* – Madame Delaunay discovered, among other things, those abstract ornaments that are so indispensable to us, and which give an air of such freshness and joy to the dresses and scarves that adorn today's women of taste.

We must thank Sonia Delaunay for her constant inventiveness, the discreet gaiety which she brought to women's fashion, the agreeable way in which she covered the soft undulations of the human body with a geometrical architecture, and the rightness and unexpectedness of her colour contrasts. But at a time when the Exposition des Arts Décoratifs appears to more attentive observers as a homage from all the countries of the world to the Cubist school, we must give her our special thanks for having, in a pleasantly roundabout way, obliged the public to take an interest, against its will, in the most generous painterly manifestations of our time.

André Lhote, 1925

Rio de Janeiro Carnival, 1928

SIMULTANEOUS fabrics have their origin in the most modern painting which emerged around 1912 and which has since been developed in Paris. It is in these paintings that Mme Sonia Delaunay has discovered the elements of construction that are fundamental to her fabrics.

Fabrics had peviously been replicas of designs known for centuries, and brought back into fashion twenty years ago by the Ballets Russes. The taste for orientalism was encouraged by decorative artists such as the virtuoso Bakst, who had a major influence on fabrics and fashion.

At almost the same time, the influence of the Fauves was making its impression on weaving and prints. It was Raoul Dufy who succumbed most wholeheartedly to this influence, the trend towards highly coloured, brilliant decorations deriving directly from the Fauve school. This originated in France and its uncontested leaders were Henri Matisse, Dufy, Friesz, Rouault, among others; it generated the first signs of a new vigour in art after Impressionism and was highly influential throughout the world.

The fabrics of this period show large and highly-coloured flowers against background patterns with violent colours, different flowers intermingling, such as poppies, pansies, garlands of roses in or against a black background; in fact, all the flowers of creation, interpreted in sumptuous colours, invaded the fashion created originally by Dufy. This style dates back to the first fabrics made by P. Poiret and Bianchini in 1910.

Then came Sonia Delaunay. She has changed all that. As a dictator of contemporary art, she has given a whole new impetus to fashion and furniture. Abandoning the decorative themes which have been known and repeated over the last ten years — natural forms intepreted and distorted so as to become fabric patterns — she has launched out on a completely new kind

SONIA - DELAUNAY

of art, no longer artistic interpretation but creation. Just as we now think it old-fashioned to show a Louis XVI basket or a Chinese landscape on an outfit, it strikes us as logical – and truly human – that one should take as a starting-point architectural and organic elements which are part of contemporary life, simpler and truer, more closely connected to modern life.

It is to Sonia Delaunay that we owe this new art, which borrows nothing from the past, but which sets the stamp on our own era. She has invented a new art from the ground up, from the laws of colour discovered in 1912.

In Sonia's paintings from the same period we see the first colour-based elements, called 'simultaneous contrasts', which form the very basis and essence of this new art of colour.

Colour alone, in the way it is organized, its dimensions, the way its inter-relations are distributed across the surface of the canvas, fabric or furniture – of space in general – determines the rhythm of the forms; and these forms resemble architectural designs in colour, playing in fugal forms. These experiments, which affect fashion itself, have always interested Sonia Delaunay, who has invented a completely new kind of fashion. In her own work, these experiments began when she invented that form of figuration which is a part of her painting – in which she had long been seeking a new means of expressing volumes.

For Sonia, a dress or a coat is a section of space, arranged and designed and, in its content and dimensions, forming an organized whole according to laws which are becoming a standardization of her art.

In consequence, Mme Delaunay does not resort to outmoded decorative elements or the modes of representation of the artists already mentioned (imitation of nature or styles).

Above: Dancer in 'Endless rhythm' dress, 1923

Motif for embroidery or edging, c. 1927

**Robert Delaunay, portrait of Mme Mandel
in one of Sonia Delaunay's simultaneous dresses, 1923**

Harlequin and a fabric project, 1924–25

Form and colour are one, and therefore the choice of content depends solely on the form desired and created by the artist.

The fabric therefore becomes a highly valuable auxiliary to the composition of the outfit, and the value of these fabrics lies in the fact that Sonia considers them in relation to a particular clothing design.

Specialist designers, who normally draw up fabric designs, make what is commonly called patterns, but often they do not know the purpose of the fabric or what the fabric design will be used for. In other words, they are not in touch with the rules of fashion in general. Even if they are agreeably composed, and their patterns are successful in themselves, it is often difficult to find a practical use for them.

Mme S.D. only ever makes a fabric composition with a view to its practical use – to become an evening dress, for example, or a sports dress or a summer coat.

And to all these compositions she brings her profound knowledge of the technique used in treating the fabric, from colouring and dyeing to weaving and cutting. Her work has ceased to be mere fabric design, and has become a much more extensive science demanding much more responsibility than is normally involved in the treatment of fabrics.

Until now, fabrics were dealt with the same way as wallpaper, by the kilometer, with no conception of their future use – or at best by chance. That was up to the dress-designer. In many cases a large number of fabrics had to be cut out; this led to a great deal of waste when the flower motifs were being applied to the dress or coat.

So this is the first time that a concern with the functional structure of the material has become a part of design, manufacture and fashion.

Sonia is simultaneous. She is in the silk-workshop (or the workshop where wool is woven, or velvet made) and the dress-designer's studio all at the same time. She gives her conception a perfect creative harmony, by thinking about all the transitions between the ready-made fabric and the final garment.

She observes all the functional stages of the technique. Sometimes, through its material, a fabric inspires her to an appropriate form of colour; at another point, the purely abstract and plastic shape of a coat suggests the corresponding creation of a fabric – and by that I mean everything involved in the technique of colour and material, all at the same time. It is a highly conscientious, highly skilled, task; and one that is innate, the result of her high degree of inventive spirit. Sonia Delaunay knows the secret of her art: simultaneity is her trademark, the mark of her mind. She has brought her inventiveness to such a pitch that she is currently winning plaudits everywhere, her fabrics have been accepted by the largest dress-designing firms in Paris; her concept is hugely successful wherever new ideas are in demand. Fashion is synonymous with innovation, and Sonia is the major innovator currently enriching the art of our time. For ten years we have been waiting for a real innovation – here it is!

Robert Delaunay,
from *Du Cubisme à l'art abstrait*, 1923

Sonia Delaunay-Terk
Costume, porté par
Gaby
Au Petit Casino
Madrid 1919

'AROUND 1911', Sonia Delaunay wrote, 'I had the idea of making, for my new-born son, a bed-cover made up of bits of fabric like the ones I had seen Russian peasants using. When it was finished, the arrangement of the pieces of material had a Cubist look to them, and we then tried to apply the process to other objects and to paintings.'[1] Thus, within a few months, an adventure had begun, which was to lead Sonia Delaunay to give a true meaning to decorative art by putting at the disposal of everyday life, in the simplest way in the world, her huge talent as a creative painter. As Bernard Dorival stresses: 'No one during those years between 1910 and 1930 was able to bring the so-called minor arts to the heights of major art, which the mistakes of the Renaissance and the centuries that followed had, alas, brought into decline.'[2] Her first works were covers for the poems of her friends Blaise Cendrars and Guillaume Apollinaire, lampshades, waistcoats worn by her husband Robert Delaunay, René Crevel and Jacques Doucet, hats, 'vollettes' and dresses. The poets composed rhymes on her dresses, occasionally with a critical irony, and Apollinaire wrote: 'On Thursdays and Sundays, you have to go to Bullier's to see Monsieur and Madame Robert Delaunay, who are busy instituting the reform of clothing.'[3] Reformers they might have been, but above all they were innovators, and we must quite definitely see the vision of a modern painter in Sonia's creations. In fact, what the artist sought to bring to everyday life was not only her innate sense of colour variations, but also her husband's experiments, in which she was closely involved, and which led Robert, from 1912, to sketch out 'a kind of painting which would be technically based on colour alone',[4] and the rhythms produced by the variations of that colour, which thus became the object, form, sensation, emotion and the profound poetry of his paintings.

Above: group of women, drawing in Indian ink, 1923 (Coll. JD/PR, Paris)

Below: dress design in blue ink, 1923 (Coll. Patrick Raynaud)

But although during the years leading up to the First World War Sonia Delaunay was designing embroidery and making clothes (they were made on the basis of samples supplied by Robert's tailor), she appears to have done so solely for the pleasure of seeing the triumph of her ideas and intuitions as a resolutely abstract painter, on her own person and in her own surroundings. And it was not until 1920, when the Russian Revolution had cut off the income on which the household had lived, that she decided to return to her previous creations and commercialize them in various ways.

In 1923, Sonia Delaunay received a major order for fabric designs from a silk-manufacturer in Lyons, and later she was to make several more series of dress-designs for a Dutch factory and for several American fashion houses. But the following year she opened her own studio in the Boulevard Malesherbes, in the apartment where they had just taken up residence. She engaged a number of women to work for her and created her first embroidered fabrics. Made on a light frame, generally in cotton, they were executed in the 'point du jour' invented by Sonia, and which may be compared to what we call 'point de Hongrie', with its wools or silks in graded and nuanced colours, greens, browns and greys mixed with striking blacks and whites. With their contrast of rigorous geometrical forms and colours, they were enormously successful, and these embroidered fabrics were used to make the famous jackets and coats worn by Gloria Swanson, the wives of Stokowski and Paul Guillaume as well as the wives of the German architects Mendelsohn, Gropius and Breuer.

In view of the success that these fabrics brought her, and in order to distribute her creations more widely, Sonia Delaunay decided during 1924 to have her first printed fabrics published, with the following note along the edge: 'Sonia Delaunay — Atelier simultané', thus affirming the wish of the artist not to dissociate her decorative work from her work as a painter, which was to remain her chief activity. Moreover, the artist made her designs from gouaches by no means inferior in quality to her painted works. Proof beyond question is supplied by the fact that the gouaches and the paintings were often shown side by side without prejudice in favour of either. Primarily a

**Nancy Cunard in a
Sonia Delaunay coat**

**Models dressed by Sonia Delaunay posing
in front of the Delaunays' Talbot, 1928**

colourist, Sonia Delaunay first of all designed her fabrics, using two, three or four colours, or more rarely five or six, in a violent chromaticism made up of the contrast of midnight blue, cherry red, black, white, yellow or green, and then imagined the different possibilities for each dress-design, involving infinite variations and colour modifications. So as to preserve the totality of the colour language and its variations and contrasts, the form is rigorous, simple, geometrical – squares, triangles and discs, crossing and intermingling, sometimes circles or lines, but always arranged with the strictest discipline. For in her fabrics as in her painting, Sonia Delaunay never took the easy way out, a memory, she said, of her drawing teacher in Germany when she was a girl, 'which will leave its mark for ever by forcing her to have a constructive basis, thus lending greater force to visual expression and banishing chance and vagueness'.[5]

In 1925, Sonia Delaunay took part in the Exposition des Arts Décoratifs on the Pont Alexandre III, with a stand that she shared with the couturier Jacques Heim. Robert invented for them an ingenious system of presentation which allowed the fabrics to move. The French and foreign press cited Sonia's works as the most interesting in the exhibition, and in *L'Art Vivant* of 1 April we read: 'printed fabrics and embroidered fabrics obey a single principle: the balance of volumes and colour. Here is the kingdom of abstraction, a constant but flexible geometry, vivid and elevated by the elation of its inspiration, by the capricious play of the brush, the triumphant joy of colour.' The same year the Librairie des Arts Décoratifs published an album entitled: *Sonia Delaunay, ses peintures, ses objects, ses tissus simultanés, ses modes*, with a text by André Lhote, and poems by Cendrars, Delteil, Tzara and Soupault who joined in paying homage to the creative spirit of both the painter and the designer. Finally, on 27 January 1927, Sonia Delaunay gave a lecture at the Sorbonne, in the highly respected Visual Arts department run by Maurice Raybal, entitled 'The Influence of Painting on the Art of Clothing', in which she spoke of the upheavals that had occurred in painting from Impressionism onwards, and which were to bring about equally irreversible changes in the field of fashion and fabric design. We should also add that the

Dress, drawing in Indian ink, 1924

artist's geometrical motifs were bought throughout the world, and are repeated and copied to this very day. They had a considerable influence and, miraculously, they never went out of fashion, and even in our own time they look contemporary, even avant-garde.

In 1930, France began to feel the repercussions of the American Depression; some admirers of Robert Delaunay expressed an interest in his work, and Sonia decided to close her studio and devoted herself exclusively to painting from then on. Thus, by the time she returned exclusively to painting, she had been enriched by a twofold experience. On the one hand she had brought her art into the street, deriving her decorative talent from her experiments in painting, related to those of her husband; but even more than this – thanks to those daily 'scales', her fabrics – she had extended the immense possibilities involved in relating different tones to one another within the most elementary forms; this was later to allow her to simplify and synthesize her own vision to attain the perfection of a pictorial language based solely on the poetics of colour.

Maïten Bouisset, 1969
(Diplômé de l'Ecole du Louvre)

Notes

(1) S. Delaunay, 'Collages de S. et R. Delaunay', in *XXe Siècle*, No. 6, Paris, 1956
(2) B. Dorival, Preface to the R. and S. Delaunay Exhibition, National Gallery of Canada, Ottawa, 1965
(3) G. Apollinaire, 'Les Réformateurs du Costume', in *Mercure de France*, No. 397, Paris, January 1914
(4) R. Delaunay, 'Du Cubisme à l'art abstrait', *Cahiers Inédits de R. Delaunay* published by P. Francastel, S.E.V.P.E.M., Paris, 1957
(5) S. Delaunay, Autobiographical text, Catalogue de la Rétrospective Sonia Delaunay au Musée National d'Art Moderne, Paris, 1967–1968

**Fabric designs,
drawings in Indian ink, 1926**

SURROUNDED by Empire and Directoire furniture in a fifteenth-century house on the Rue des Grands Augustins, we arrived with our stockpile of revolutionary paintings. Delaunay, after the Neo-Impressionist period, discovered the importance of Cézanne, and from 1909 onwards he painted the Saint-Séverins, the 'Villes' and the Eiffel Towers. His broken Eiffel Towers which artistically shook the stability of the old world to its very foundations.

As for myself, in line with my experiments in free painting, I was painting portraits inspired by Van Gogh.

Finding myself in that equivocal position between our own present and the things that surrounded us, I instinctively set about putting white calico on the walls, since our paintings harmonized more successfully with this than they did with the Directoire wallpaper.

At the same time, making use of a collection of samples of multicoloured fabrics given to me by my husband's tailor, I felt the need to make a dress to correspond to the paintings we were doing. That was in 1913. The beginning of Cubism. I had already made collages on books and the Trans-Siberian Railway, and this 'simultaneous' dress was in perfect harmony with the art we were making at the time. (See the poem by Blaise Cendrars: 'On the dress she has a body').

From that point on, my dresses were designed in accordance with the female form.

When, in 1922–23, the silk-makers of Lyons asked me to make fifty designs for them, I realized after a moment of hesitation that I would be making colour studies that would correspond to my art. (Studies which I was later able to use in the development of colour relations, and in breaking thoroughly new ground in painting.)

Various fashion models, c. 1923/26

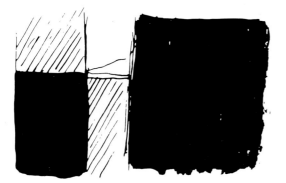

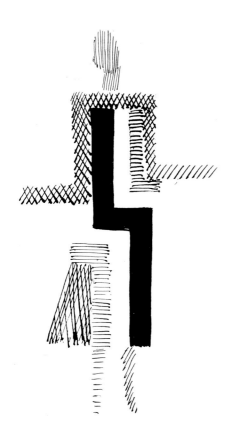

My fabrics were hugely successful, particularly from 1925 onwards. I also designed hand-made tapestries for coats.

All these works were made for women, and all were constructed in relation to the body. They were not copies of paintings transposed on to women's bodies, as one couturier has done with Mondrian and Op Art. Painters who base their work on the principles of optics copy scientific illustrations and produce them in endless variations without giving so much as a thought to their use as clothing. Besides, I wrote in 1925:

'I consider the sonority and the visual movement of colours virgin territory from the point of view of the visual arts.' I wrote that because we were studying the independent lives that colours acquired when we liberated them from subject-matter.

That is why, when contemporary painters expound woolly theories about Pop Art and the like, without knowing which direction they should take and only wanting to shock people with eccentricities – flattening cars and things of that kind – they are not serious; all they are doing is providing a form of society entertainment. The field is open for anyone willing to take the trouble level-headedly to continue in a new direction, examining the independent life of each colour in relation to the colours surrounding it, and here there are infinite discoveries to be made.

As to the Mondrian dresses, or those made after Vasarely or other eccentrics, I find all that completely ridiculous. It's a promotional medium, but it isn't a basis for either development or construction: it's circus. That's why they're turning to the experiments I did between 1923 and 1930 in women's fashions, and copying my experiments rather than understanding and developing them by adapting them to contemporary life.

That's a field that belongs to everybody.

Clever people have made hundreds of millions with my idea – using it as a basis for off-the-peg clothes.

Letter from Sonia Delaunay to Jacques Damase, May 1968,
published in *Jardin des Modes*, April 1980

**Dress and group,
drawings in Indian ink, 1925**

47 **Gouache painting of swimmer, 1929**

1928

1928

48-50 **Three swimsuit designs, 1928**

1928

51-53 **Swimsuits and accessories in printed fabrics, 1928**

1509

Sonia Delaunay
Projet Affiche Petrol

Sonia Delaunay

m-558

nº 68

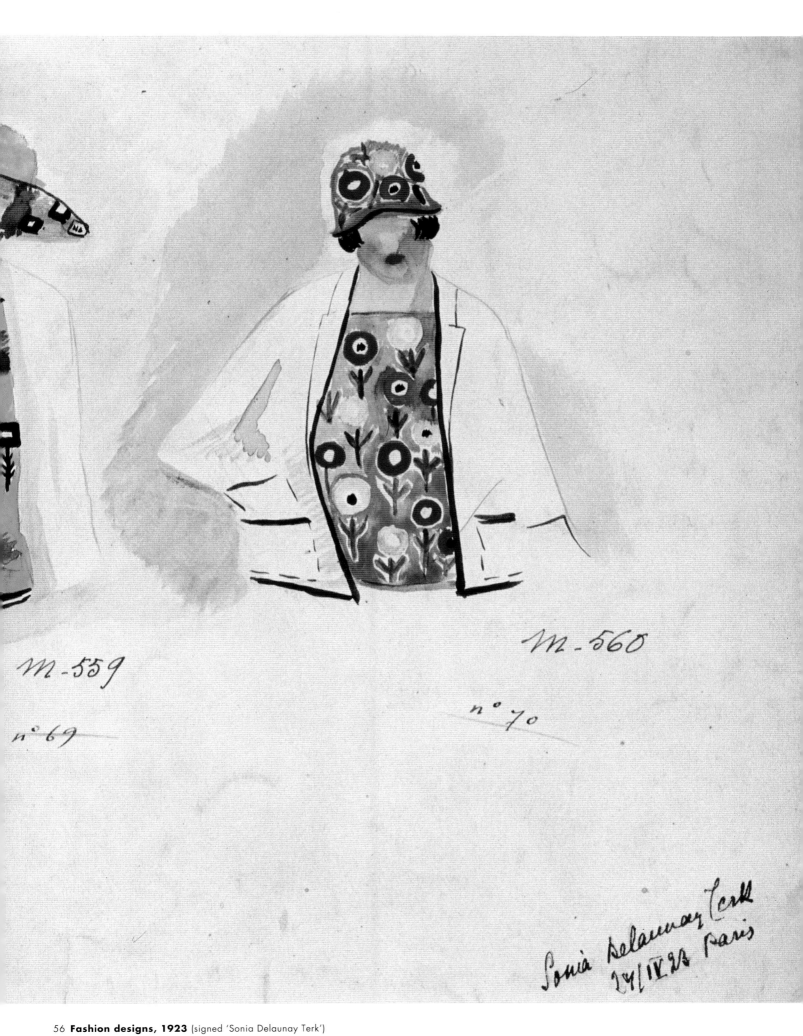

M-559

n° 69

M-560

n° 70

Sonia Delaunay Terk
27/IX 23 Paris

56 **Fashion designs, 1923** (signed 'Sonia Delaunay Terk')

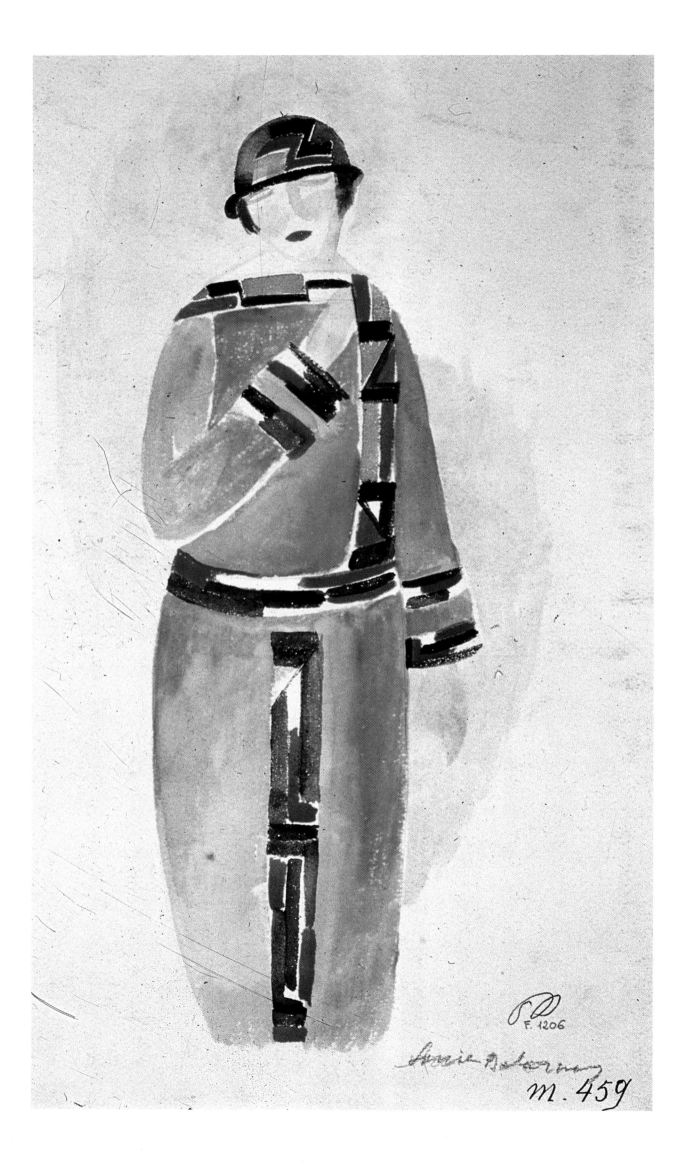

F. 1206

Sonia Delaunay

m. 459

57 **Dress design, 1923**

58 **Jacket design, 1923**

60 **Coat design, 1923**

59 **Coat for Gloria Swanson, 1923**

61,62 **Ballet costume designs, 1924**

4 saisons
(Hiver)
Sonia Delaunay
1924

63 **'Poem dress', 1922**

64 **Evening gown design, 1922**

65 **Design for peignoir, 1922**

66 **Dress design, 1924**

67, 68
**Two scarf designs,
1925, 1927/28**

253 H

1927/28

69 **Design for evening gown, 1926**

70 **Rio carnival design, 1928**

F 1218 A

71,72 **Two dress designs, 1923/28**

73,74 **Rio carnival designs, 1928**

75 **Scarf with discs, 1924**

76 'Dancers', 1923

77 **Play by Tristan Tzara, costumes by SD, 1923**

78 **Rio carnival design, 1928**

79 **'Tops', Rio carnival designs, 1928**

THE modernism of these fabrics is such that some of them have recently been reissued, and the spirit they reveal has been a great inspiration to artists and fashion-designers. As we know, Sonia Delaunay's work has been one of the admitted sources of Op Art.

Some of them derive from older works, from the book-covers made between 1913 and 1914 for an edition of Cendrars' collection *Pâques* and a collection of the journal *Der Sturm*, for example, putting their original conception before 1920. Others are similar to covers for magazines such as *Les Arts Plastiques*.[1] But Sonia Delaunay always respects the specific character of the design for clothing fabrics: simple and clear motifs, the way they fit the body, colours which are often vivid, but which harmonize most agreeably.

In her fabric designs, Sonia Delaunay, who had already proved to be a great colourist before 1914, allowed her sense of colour, freed from all constraints, to mature into the basis for a pictorial language. It should be stressed that the style of these fabrics is not so much a digression as an essential stage in the development of her art (the artist called them her 'scales'). Having shown herself to be an instinctive colourist in her first Fauvist canvases, she laid the foundations for this language in the series of works painted between 1913 and 1914 (*Le Bal Bullier* and *Prismes Eléctriques*), which take as their starting-point the study of the colours cast by artificial lighting. The later works are paintings that make use of this colour language, whose vague possibilities and richness appeared and blossomed in the divine music of the gouaches and abstract canvases of the last twenty years. And many more recent artists have borrowed elements of this language.

Charleston, drawing in Indian ink, 1925

In another respect, Sonia Delaunay's fabrics reveal an essential aspect of her character: like Robert Delaunay, she was always concerned with bringing modern art out of the confines of traditional easel-painting. There is nothing that penetrates life more thoroughly than fabrics and fashion, and we know that, not content with creating fabric designs, she also designed thousands of items of clothing: clothes for the city or the beach, whimsical clothes and dance and theatre costumes. She was also one of the first avant-garde painters to make costumes for the cinema. More generally, at every stage in her career Sonia Delaunay always made works which could be circulated among the public in a way that paintings cannot be, because they played a part in everyday life and could be made in large numbers: murals for the 1937 exhibition, book illustrations, book-covers, lampshades, tapestries, stained-glass, engravings, and, most recently, a pack of cards and the decoration of a sports-car (Matra 530).

Thus, the thousands of fabrics designed by Sonia Delaunay, which were very successful in their own right and major milestones in the history of fabrics, were not simply occasional pieces. Both in their style and their purpose, they held an integral place in the artist's concerns, and amount to an essential element in her *oeuvre*.

Michel Hoog,
Curator at the Musée National d'Art Moderne, Paris, 1969

[1] Catalogue for the exhibition at the Musée National d'Art Moderne, No. 122

Scarf and fabric design (Op Art), 1933

**Left: Silk fabric printed for Chanel
(there are variants), 1925**

IT would appear that throughout the history of the development of printed fabrics the great artists, the greatest artists, gave this form of expression the cold shoulder, since it had always been relegated to a sub-category of the so-called minor or applied arts. This must account for their lack of interest. In addition, the industry has a short history in Europe, dating back only to the seventeenth century. One of the reasons why printing on fabrics occupied a low position in the eyes of the great traditional artists, despite the fact that it was highly successful in the field of clothing, was that the fabric used was cotton. Silk was the only textile considered truly noble throughout the whole of the *ancien régime*. It alone was seen as worth dyeing, and thus became the prerogative of major artists. The use of wool in tapestries meant that it too was placed on a pedestal. In fact, in the great ceremonial suites of kings and princes, the furniture fabrics were always silk for the curtains, chairs and sofas, and wool and silk for tapestries. Cotton, when it was used in furniture, was always relegated to the smaller suites.

In the eighteenth century one artist alone broke this rule: Jean-Baptiste Huet. In the field of fabric printing in France, Huet was the first artist to lend the industry some nobility. And he is still not considered a genius: Oudry, Boucher, Leprince, his masters and contemporaries, dedicated themselves to tapestry only in connection with the workshops at Beauvais, Gobelins or la Savonnerie, just like Huet himself.

But most print-designers – and many of them were fine – were simply pleasant, amiable, sometimes gifted, artisans. Mademoiselle Jouannon (commonly called Charlotte), Bossert, Perrier at Jouy, Jean-Henri Dollfus, M.B. Lebert, and Malaine, for example, and others from Mulhouse, fall into this category. They were all content for a long time simply to imitate imported

**Various fabric motifs,
1925, 1945, 1966**

Indian and Persian designs. They did not stray from the tried and tested tradition of floral decoration drawn from the ornamental language of the Middle East and Far East. This tradition was also maintained throughout the nineteenth century. Thus the cashmere launched by Mulhouse, along with Paisley in Scotland, which enjoyed a great deal of success around the middle of the last century, was merely a reprise and elaboration of a much older motif.

But under the aegis of Oberkampf at Jouy there was a trend in print designs close to that started by Sonia Delaunay: the tendency towards geometry and abstraction, which proved short-lived because of its lack of success. All these fabrics, using greys, ochres and blacks, were made for the women of the people. But they too preferred the fresher, more colourful patterns of 'mignonettes' or 'bonnes herbes'. The general atmosphere was not, even under the Directoire and the Empire, in favour of fabrics with geometrical patterns, although the designs were often fairly surprising in their search for a certain degree of modernism. In a short span of time, Oberkampf, always in financial difficulties, had to throw in the towel and go back to traditional methods. But there is something brilliant about his original artistic creations, even though their treatment of colour lacks intensity. Colour would only come into its own a short time later.

Soon after 1810, in fact, Mulhouse, with its many design studios and, more particularly, its laboratories, was to give a new direction to printmaking with the use of colour, employing a brilliant and heightened polychromy. A short time previous to this, in 1807, the chemist Chaptal had published a treatise which was to capture the imagination of the Mulhouse printmakers: 'The Art of Dyeing Cotton Red'. This was to be the great era of

madder, for almost half a century. In the fabrics of this period Alsatian polychromy revealed unprecedented courage and taste. But it is a shame that, in this instance as well, the absolutely splendid and brightly coloured materials were intended primarily for popular taste; they quickly became routine and lacking in creativity. The designs and colours were drawn primarily from the ornamental language of the people: stylized flowers, borders and bouquets on a red background. Prior to 1925, this era was the only one which dared assert itself in a range of pure colours.

In the 1900s, Art Nouveau was to give a new lift to printing on fabrics, at the very least bringing a new richness to polychromy, which had degenerated to a very low level, and creating new non-traditional designs. The printed fabric during this period was starting to find a new vocation, but it was not yet to attain genius. In the nineteenth century, and right up to 1914, not a single serious artist was willing to take an interest in printed fabrics. Thanks to the highly advanced state of the various techniques inolved, this had become a high-yield industrial and commercial product with which artists had ceased to have any affinity. Although the prints of the last century are excellently produced, they are still – apart from a few exceptions – distressingly poor in their use of of colour, their designs and their conception.

This progressive dulling in the field of fabric printing was only saved at the last minute by the revelation of Serge Diaghilev's Ballets Russes, with gleaming stage-sets and costumes by a whole constellation of painters including Sonia Delaunay. This turning point occurred around 1907–11, and matchless artists were to bring about a renaissance in fabrics, introducing a fresh vigour to their design and colour. A new age of artistic glory and richness was dawning. Of these artists, Sonia Delaunay – more even than

Above: Indian ink drawing, 1966

Right: project for a carpet, c. 1925

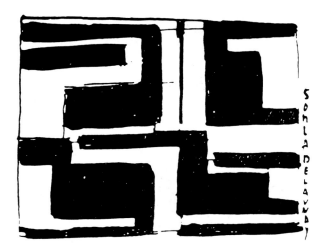

Dufy — gave an unparalleled originality and novelty to her fabrics. She was, moreover, one of the few artists to see a printed fabric as a work of art in its own right and to accord it the same pictorial and artistic value as painting.

Her studies for fabric designs, which she collected in exercise books and still guards jealously, are a true bible of contemporary abstract art. They reveal a large number of different variations and fundamental experiments in the new art, in which poetry also played an important part.

After all, this new trend, born out of Cubism and created by Sonia and Robert Delaunay, bore the name of 'simultanisme' after Blaise Cendrars, and even 'orphisme', after Guillaume Apollinaire.

J.M. Tuchscherer, 1970

Right: Endless rhythm, c. 1960

Below: project for a scarf, c. 1925

IN the *Mercure de France* of 1 January 1914, Guillaume Apollinaire wrote: 'You have to go to Bullier's, to see Monsieur and Madame Robert Delaunay, who are busy bringing about the reform of clothing. Simultaneous Orphism has produced sartorial novelties that are not to be sneezed at. They would have given Carlyle a curious chapter in *Sartor Resartus*. M. and Mme Delaunay are innovators. They are unencumbered by the imitation of old styles, and as they wish to be of their time they are not attempting to make any innovations in the shape of the cut, but are rather trying to influence it by using the new and infinitely varied material of colours.

'Here, for example, is a suit by M. Robert Delaunay: violet jacket, beige waistcoat, dark-brown trousers. And here is another one: red coat with a blue collar, red socks, black and yellow shoes, black trousers, green jacket, sky-blue waistcoat, tiny red tie. . . . Here is the description of a simultaneous dress by Mme Delaunay: violet suit, long violet and green belt and, under the jacket, a blouse divided into areas of bright, delicate or faded colours, combining old rose, tangerine, '*nattier*' blue, scarlet, etc., appearing in juxtaposition on different materials such as woollen cloth, taffeta, tulle, flannelette, moiré and matt silk.

'Such variety has not gone unnoticed. It lends fantasy to elegance.

'And if, having gone to Bullier's, you do not see them immediately, you should be aware that these clothing-reformers are generally to be found below the orchestra, studying, without a hint of scorn, the monotonous clothes of the dancing men and women . . .'

In 1923, a firm of silk-manufacturers in Lyons ordered 50 fabric designs from her. This is how abstract geometrical design was introduced into printed fabrics. [. . .]

**Various fabric motifs,
1925, 1945, 1966**

Scarves, ballet costumes, embroidered waistcoats made specially for Jacques Doucet or René Crevel, embroidered coats, were quickly to follow. All this work was presented at the fashion-centre of the Bal Bullier in 1923; a total collage, since everything there was a collage, from the floor-covering to the ceiling, via the outfits of the models.

For a freer woman, involved in work, playing sports and dancing, a practical fashion was required; it ignored the waist and the bosom, shortened the skirt, invented pyjamas and cut the hair short. These were the women that men found on their return from the war: companions with neat and intentionally youthful figures, with a masculine air that was surprising but which presented a new attraction, that of the *garçonne*.

This development in clothes-design did not meet with the full acceptance of *haute couture*, which soon lost its stranglehold over its clientèle. Within a few years, fashion houses such as Doucet, Doeuillet and Drecoll closed (for Paul Poiret, his 1925 barges were also his swansong), while others were starting up. Women's names dominated the revitalization of Parisian elegance, and this was one of the chief characteristics of the period: alongside Mme Gerver, Mme Paquin, Jeanne Lanvin, Madeleine Vionnet and Chanel, who were to occupy centre-stage for the next twenty years, we find the fashion-house of Sonia Delaunay.

If, in general, ornamentation in clothing was to lose its richness, the fabrics were still highly experimental from a technical point of view. Alongside a fashion for matt or shining satin there were new materials, such as *crêpe georgette*, muslin with a metal border, tartan, etc.

When Baudelaire wrote his famous line: *Je hais le mouvement qui déplace les lignes*, he could hardly have expected that the taste of

Group of women, drawing in Indian ink, 1925

contemporary poets and artists would be directed towards forms in motion. At the 1924 Salon d'Automne, there was a simultaneous cinematic presentation of fabrics . . .

'When you look,' Apollinaire continues, 'as you pass through the stands that adorn the vast hall of the Grand Palais, what attracts the eye is the particular appearance of that mobile stand adorned by the fabrics of Sonia Delaunay. All that movement undeniably produces, on the retina first of all, a new appeal to which you are unaccustomed. Then your mind grows anxious . . . particularly because, almost at the same time, you notice other stands nearby where it seems, in contrast, that you have been spirited off to the Musée Grévin, a date for the natural historian . . . Of course I am not talking about the cadavers, the paintings on the first floor and all over the place. Might this not be the first scene from Delteil's novel: *La peste à Paris dans les cinq sens?* . . .'

In reaction to the black and white which was still *de rigueur*, the influence of the pre-war period returned in the taste for rich materials and violent tones in evening dresses as well as capes and scarves. In his creations, Paul Poiret preserved the exuberance of vivid and 'solid' colours launched fifteen years earlier by Serge Diaghilev's Ballets Russes. Poiret surrounded himself with artists such as Paul Iribe and Raoul Dufy.

'But short, flat, geometrical, rectangular, women's clothing took the parallelogram as its template, and 1925 will not welcome the return of a fashion of soft curves, a proud breast, succulent hips,' Colette wrote in *Vogue*. Reduced to its most basic lines, this vision was quite precise, and provided a good definition of couture as it appeared to the astonished viewers in certain paintings by Braque or Picasso, in which they were at pains to make out where the painter had intended to place the torso and the legs.

But Sonia Delaunay's experiments were quite different: she did not use colour in the way Poiret recommended; in her work, the violence of the colour was not gratuitous; she did not construct Cubist or Futurist outfits, but, quite rationally, dresses and coats which betrayed her vision neither as a painter nor as a woman. [. . .]

Nancy Cunard, design for a coat, drawing in Indian ink, 1923 (Coll. J. Damase, Paris)

**Sonia Delaunay models in front of a tree sculpture in concrete
by the architect Robert Mallet-Stevens, 1925**

In her lecture at the Sorbonne, Sonia Delaunay said that she intended to adapt fashion to women's real-life requirements, but that all her imagination, all the richness of her vision, was given free rein on the surface of a fabric. We should not underestimate the influence of the Exposition des Arts Décoratifs held in Paris in 1925, which particularly granted the artistic and luxury industries of Paris their first major opportunity since the war to show their wares. Like all international exhibitions, this one opened in confusion on 18 July 1925. It was also nicknamed *L'exposition des Arts Décor Hâtifs*, because '1925 still had a whiff of *fin-de-siècle* about it', according to Armand Lanoux. [. . .]

When President Doumergue paid his official visit, he was slightly lost. Black music, the pearl of the diamond-merchants' pavilion; reinforced concrete by Mallet-Stevens; major stores with art studios — Pomone with its padding, Primavera with its *négritude*, the mastery of the Galeries Lafayette, Style Gomina with the ideal apartment of *Lewis and Irène*.

On his barges, *Amor, délice et orgue*, commodore Paul Poiret was waiting for the presidential guest, who was walking, walking, walking among the high-society fountains, Dunand's lacquer-work, Rodier's fabrics, Cartier's jewellery, Baguès's chandeliers and Hermès's leathers. 'Of the stands on the Pont Alexandre III,' wrote Lanoux, 'the journalists considered Sonia Delaunay's to be by far the best, exhibiting her "simultaneous" fabrics and admirable embroideries, all with the same spirit of balance and colourful harmony.' These sumptuous coats with their fine nuances, like a reflection of autumnal splendours or the delicacy of early-morning mists, were made for the shoulders of royalty. She also worked with furs in a quite individual way, bringing out their neutral tones with astonishing virtuosity; she mixed furs and embroidery, metal and wool or silk, but she only ever used metal with certain matt tones, stressings its rich and discreet elegance.

These were simultaneous materials, materials considered not at rest, wrote Delteil, but moving as one motion among many, interlocking and echoing the dynamic conception of the universe . . . Her 1925 album had just been published. In *Les Nouvelles Littéraires*, Florent Fels hailed it in these

Model in printed silk pyjamas, 1927

Business card of the 'Boutique Simultanée', 1925

boutique
« simultané »
n° 16
pont alexandre III
aux
arts décoratifs

1925

sonia delaunay

tissus simultanés brevetés
modèles art simultané
modes broderie déposées

PARIS : 19, boulevard malesherbes, tél. élysées 10-88
LONDON : PARIS - trades, 20 a, berkeley street
RIO de JANEIRO casa de aladin rua 13 de maio 52

terms: 'I know that when I open it I shall find the whole singing range of the vivid colours of one of the most prodigious creators of our time. I use the word "creator" intentionally because since the art of designers such as Alexandre Benois and Bakst brought a new attitude towards stage-design, and the extravaganzas of the Ballets Russes have in turn made way for a decade of sartorial art, Sonia Delaunay's art is currently bringing a new youthfulness to fashion and the art of decoration.'

As they awaited this spectacle, painters and poets said that Sonia Delaunay's colour relations were poetry. A poetry with a sense of usefulness, a decoration made with the most simple means: a few tones and geometrical forms, married together, strong tones juxtaposed and coordinated in ravishing harmonies with a rare skill.

And they are dress-designs, fabric maquettes, cloths, but so rich that they are as delightful as a sumptuous spectacle. 'The simultaneous fragments,' as Robert Delaunay concisely put it, 'originated in the most modern painting which first saw light around 1912 and subsequently developed in Paris.' It was in these paintings that Sonia Delaunay discovered the elements that formed a constructive basis for her fabrics.

Jacques Damase

**Above: Dress design,
ink drawing, 1926
(Coll. JD/PR)**

**Below: signature stamped on
the edging of Sonia Delaunay fabrics**

**Right: Façade of the 'Boutique
simultanée' at the 1925
Art Deco exposition in Paris**

GILBERT GIRAU—
SONIA DELAU
NAY
SIMULTANÉ
HEIM
FURS
MAROQUINERIE

The angel has slipped his hand
into the basket, the eye of the fruit.
He arrests the wheels of the motor cars
and the human heart's dizzy gyroscope.

Tristan Tzara 1923

**Dress-poem by Tristan Tzara,
gouache, 1923**

F. 1514.

Sonia Delaunay 1925

80 **Fabric motif, 1925**

81 **Model in suit designed by SD, 1926**

82,83 **Printed fabric and gouache design for same fabric (as worn by the model)**

84 **Scarf design, 1943**

85 **Harlequin fabric design, 1923**

86, 87 **Sports coat and (right) the material from**
which it was made, 1926

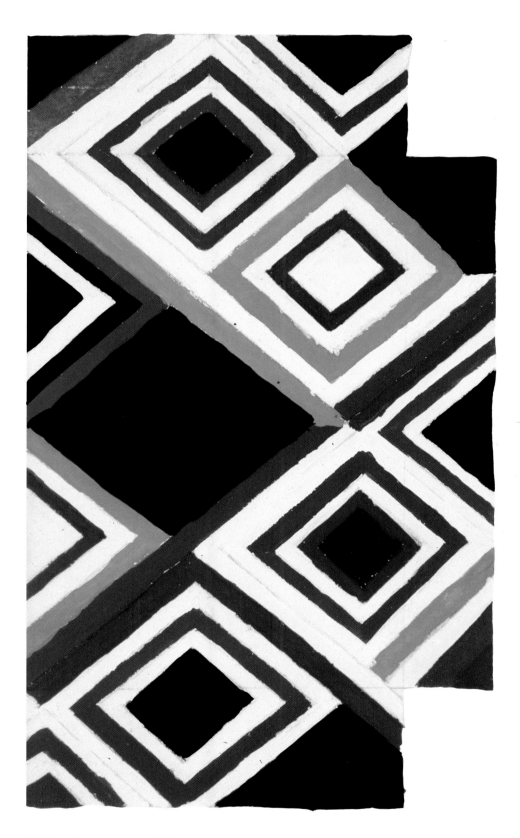

89 **Handbag design, c. 1926**

88 **Motif called 'African'
or 'African art', 1926**
(opposite)

90,91 **Silk printed with diamonds and squares, *c.* 1926**

92 (page 132-133) **Variant of the diamonds/squares design**

93,94 **Two handbag designs, 1925**

95 **Printed silk fabric, 1926**

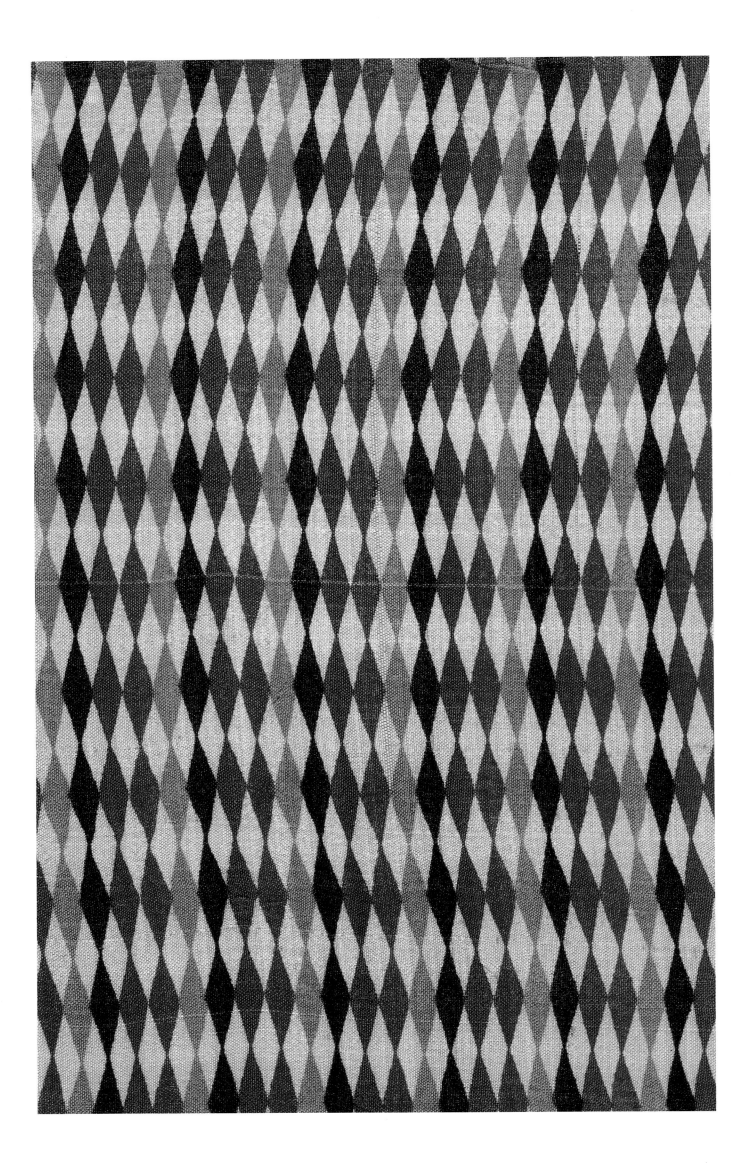

96
Printed linen fabric

97-98
**Dress (1924) and
handbag design**

100 **Fabrics and designs by SD shown in Paris Art Déco exhibition, 1925**

101,102 **Two embroidered handbag designs**

103 **Printed silk, 1926**

104 **Fringed coat in embroidered
     wool, 1924**

105 (overleaf) **Design for the famous fabric No. 6, 1923** ▶

n: 106

106

106 **Printed silk** (left)

107 **Suit design, 1925**

108 **SD monogram fabric design, 1928**

109 **Rio carnival design, 1928**

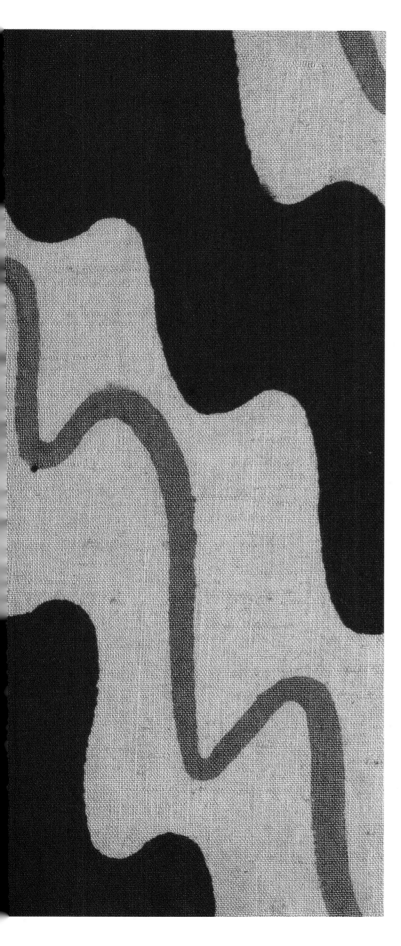

110,111 **Printed linen fabric and a beach coat made of the same fabric, 1925**

152

203

112 **Design for furnishing fabric, 1928**

113 **Evening gown with spiral motif, 1926**

114 **Printed silk with spiral motif**

116, 117 **Two dresses of fabrics with similar motif, 1925**

118, 119 **Printed silk and cotton, 1925**

120 **'Lady Blue' design, 1924**

121 **Pleated dress in printed tulle, 1925**

122 **Floral design, 1925** (opposite)

123
Printed silk
(opposite)

124,125
**Design for an
embroidered
handbag, and
printed tulle
with similar
motif, 1924**

126
'Top' costume for Rio carnival,
1927/70

127, 128
Two fabric designs in gouache

129
(overleaf) **Floral design,
printed linen, 1926**

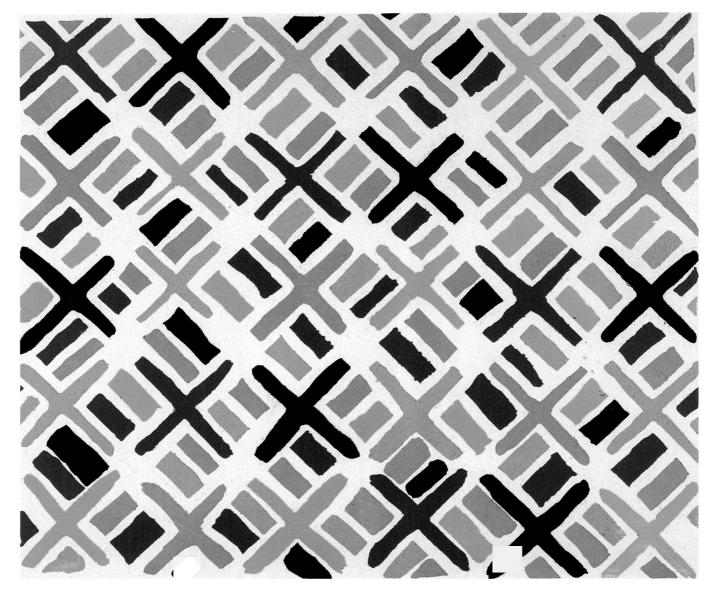

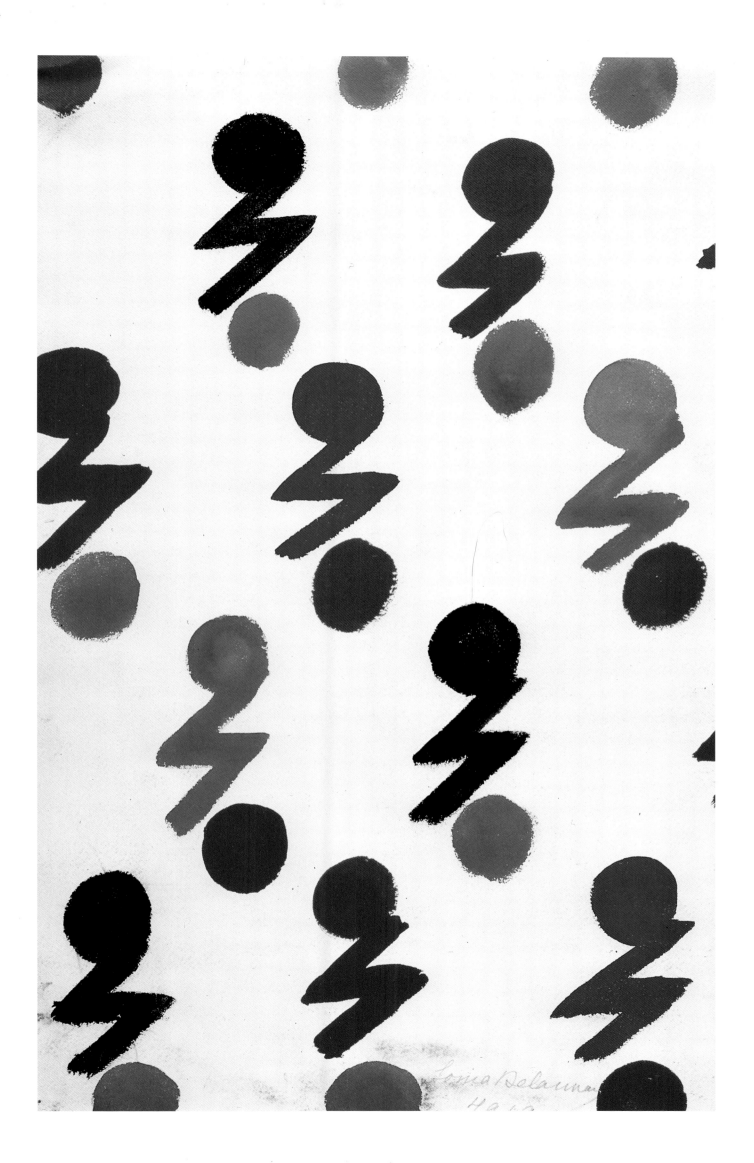

130 **SD, c. 1970, wearing scarf of her own design and
standing in front of various of her paintings**

1885	14 November, birth of Sophie Stern in Gradizhsk, Ukraine
1890	adopted by maternal uncle, Henri Terk, a lawyer in St Petersburg. Spends childhood and adolescence there; vacations in Finland and visits to Switzerland and Italy
1903–05	studies with Ludwig Schmid-Reutte in Karlsruhe (Arnold Schoenberg also a student here)
1905	arrival in Paris; attends Académie de la Palette, where she meets the artists Ozenfant, Segonzac, Boussingault Learns engraving around 1905–06
1907	Fauve period; influence of Van Gogh and Gauguin
1908	marriage of convenience in London with the German critic and collector Wilhelm Uhde Exhibits at the Galerie Notre-Dame-des-Champs, Paris
1910	divorces Uhde and marries Robert Delaunay. They move into 3, rue des Grands-Augustins, where they keep a studio until 1935
1911	executes her first abstract work, a cover in appliqué fabric for the cradle of her son Charles, born this year
1912	first fabrics of 'simultaneous contrasts', first simultaneous collages, book bindings and clothes
1913	the Delaunays become friends of Blaise Cendrars. Trip to Berlin with Cendrars and Apollinaire on occasion of RD's exhibit at Herwarth Walden's 'Der Sturm' Gallery (lecture by Apollinaire on 'Orphism') Lecture by Smirnoff in St Petersburg on RD's 'Simultaneous Contrasts' Studies of light and movement: *Le Bal Bullier*; *Electric Prisms*; *Studies of Light*; *Boulevard Saint-Michel* Illustrates Cendrars' *La Prose du Transsibérien et de la Petite Jehanne de France* Participates with RD in the first German Salon d'Automne in Berlin at 'Der Sturm' Gallery, exhibiting paintings, posters, books and other simultaneous objects Creates simultaneous dresses and vests
1914	numerous poster projects Inspired by her simultaneous dresses, Cendrars dedicates to her the poem *Sur la robe elle a un corps* Vacation in Spain Delaunays move to Madrid; influenced by the light and colours of Spain
1915–16	period of the *Portuguese Still-lifes* and *The Market* in Minho, Portugal Study of dance movements (tango, flamenco)
1916	self-portrait as cover illustration for the catalogue of her exhibition at the Nya Konstgalleriet in Stockholm
1917	*The Dancers* series Russian Revolution deprives her of income Return to Madrid Thanks to her talent and connections with Diaghilev, Massine and Nijinsky, successfully launches into design and fashion Makes costumes for ballet *Cléopâtre*
1921	back in Paris, the Delaunays settle at 19, blvd Malesherbes. In this apartment, described by René Crevel in 1920, they entertain such painters as Gleizes, Lhote and Chagall; also the new literary avant-garde linked to the Dadaist and Surrealist groups. They form close friendships with Tzara, André Breton, Mayakovsky
1922	interior decoration of the Neuilly bookshop called 'Au Sans Pareil' Embroiders Philippe Soupault's curtain-poem for the blvd Malesherbes apartment Soupault dedicates 'Evening Coat' to her First dress-poems with Tzara First simultaneous scarves Bindings of works by Tzara and Iliazd (Zdanevitch)
1923	Lyons firm gives her first order for simultaneous textiles Costumes for two evenings organized by Iliazd: 'Dancer with Discs', executed by Lizica Codreano at the Licorne, and the play *Le Coeur à gaz* by Tzara (for 'The Evening of the Bearded Heart') at the Michel Théâtre Set and costumes for the 'Fashion Boutique' at the *bal travesti* 'Transmental' organized by the Union of Russian Artists
1924	produces her simultaneous fabric creations First coats in wool tapestry Costumes for the Bal Banal and for Delteil's poem 'The Coming Fashion' presented at Hôtel Claridge Exhibits her fabrics 'in motion' at the Salon d'automne
1925	takes part in the Exposition des Arts décoratifs in collaboration with couturier Jacques Heim ('Boutique Simultané' on the Pont Alexandre III)
1926	with RD creates costumes and sets for *Le P'tit Parigot* and costumes and fabrics for *Vertigo*, films by Marcel L'Herbier
1927	lecture at the Sorbonne: 'The Influence of Painting on Fashion Design'
1928	sets for Massine ballet *The Four Seasons* and costumes for the Rio de Janeiro Carnival
1929	presentation of the album *Fabrics and Carpets* Furniture for the bachelor's establishment in the film *Because I Love You*
1930	the album *Sonia Delaunay: Compositions, Couleurs, Idées*
1931	returns almost exclusively to painting
1932	publishes 'Artists and the Future of Fashion' in Jacques Heim's house journal
1933	resumes her diary begun in 1902 and interrupted in 1906, kept regularly from now on
1934	publishes 'L'Art de la devanture' (On the Art of the Shopfront) in *Présentations*
1935	Delaunays move from blvd Malesherbes to 16, rue Saint-Simon RD interested in luminous advertising and with Sonia sets up a stand at the Salon de la lumière where they present 'micatube' lamps
1936	wins the first prize for a luminous poster in the contest organized by the Paris Electric Supply Co.

1936–37	executes enormous mural paintings for the 1937 international exhibition in Paris: *Distant Travels, Portugal*, and *Airplane Engine, Propellor and Dashboard*
1938	monumental door in coloured cement for the entrance to the exhibition *Mural Art*
	First research towards designing a deck of cards
1939	first exhibition of 'New Realities' at Galerie Charpentier (first Salon of abstract art)
1941	after RD's death, joins the Arps in Grasse, where the painter Alberto Magnelli is also staying
1942–43	living in Grasse
	Executes 'works for two' with Arp and with Magnelli (lithographs published in 1950)
1944	three months stay in Toulouse, where she again meets old friends Jean Cassou, Tzara, Fels, and the Laportes
	Decoration of the International Center of the Red Cross
1945	returns to Paris
	Exhibits with the Concrete Art group at the Galerie Drouin
1946	organizes with Louis Carré the first large RD retrospective; and with Fredo Sidès, at his request, the second Salon of New Realities
1947	first studies for *The Alphabet*
	Participates in the exhibition *Tendencies of Abstract Art* at the Galerie Denise René with 20 other artists, including Arp and Hans Hartung
1948	participates in two exhibitions: *A Quarter* at the Galerie des Deux-Iles with Sophie Taeuber-Arp, Arp and Magnelli; *Abstract Tapestries and Embroideries* at Colette Allendy with Arp, Bryen and Sophie Taeuber-Arp
1949	André Farcy, curator at the Museum of Grenoble, proposes that she undertake a 'Homage to Robert Delaunay' which results in the first Masters of Abstract Art exhibition at Galerie Maeght in Paris
1950	publication of an album of 10 lithographs: *Jean Arp, Sonia Delaunay, Alberto Magnelli, Sophie Taeuber-Arp*
1951	with Cassou and Georges Salles, takes charge of the Brancusi gift to the Musée National d'art moderne, Paris
1952	member of the newly founded group *Espace*
	One-man show at Galerie Bing
	Participates henceforth in major art shows throughout the world
1954	executes mosaics exhibited in Biot
	Publishes 'Salut Blaise Cendrars' in the Lille review, *Zénith*
1956	publishes writings on her collages and those of RD in the review *XXe siècle*
	Illustrates Tzara's *Permitted Fruit* with 4 pochoir compositions
1957	executes a monumental door for truck-manufacturer Berliet at the Automobile Show
1958–59	Robert and Sonia Delaunay exhibition at Lyons Museum
1960	executes a simultaneous deck of cards issued by the Deutsche Spielkarten Museum in Bielefeld
1961	eight colour etchings for Tzara's *Juste présent*, and an album of 6 colour lithographs published by Pagani, Milan (Ed. Grattacielo)
1962	exhibits gouaches at the Galerie Denise René; publication on this occasion of an album of 6 pochoirs with poems by Rimbaud, Mallarmé, Cendrars, Delteil, Soupault and Tzara, entitled *Poetry of Words, Poetry of Colours*
	Publishes a 'Homage to Cendrars' in *Mercure de France*
1963	bequest to the Musée National d'art moderne of 117 works by Robert and Sonia Delaunay exhibited at the Louvre Museum
1964	presents her graphic research at the Pierre Bérès bookshop
1965	first 'Robert and Sonia Delaunay' exhibition in North America organized by the National Gallery of Canada, in Ottawa
	Exhibition of textile and fashion projects at the retrospective of the year 1925 at the Pavillon de Marsane
1966	publication of the book *Rhythmes-Couleurs*, poems by Jacques Damase with 11 pochoirs by Sonia Delaunay
	Executes stained-glass window for the Church of Saux in Montpézat-de-Quercy and mosiacs for the Pagani Foundation near Milan
	Gobelins executes two tapestries based on Sonia Delaunay sketches for the Mobilier national (national collection of furniture)
	Edition of an album of 6 colour engravings for Galerie Schwarz in Milan
1967	after an interruption of 30 years, new creations of rugs for Jacques Damase
	Decoration of a racing car Matra 530
	Major retrospective at the Musée National d'art moderne
1968	numerous lithographs
	Sets and costumes for Stravinsky's *Danses concertantes* presented by the Ballet Theatre of Amiens
1969	publication of *The Alphabet* and *Dress Poems* in collaboration with Jacques Damase
1970	first major exhibition of tapestries at Galerie La Demeure
	Editions XXe Siècle publishes the album of 10 colour etchings, *With Myself*
	On an official visit to the USA, President Pompidou of France presents President Richard Nixon with fabric by Sonia Delaunay
1971	first comprehensive exhibition of her textiles at the Musée de l'impression sur étoffes in Mulhouse ('Printed fabrics of the 1920s')
	Two of her tapestries are executed at Olivier Pinton in Aubusson
1972	exhibition 'Sonia and Robert Delaunay in Portugal and their friends Vianna, Souza-Cardoso, Pacheco, Almada Negreiros' at the Gulbenkian Foundation in Lisbon
	Retrospective of her tapestries at the Musée d'Art moderne de la ville de Paris
1973	receives the Grand Prize of the City of Paris
	Publication of Rimbaud's *Illuminations* illustrated with 18 pochoirs, exhibited in 1975 at the Bibliothèque Nationale with *La Prose du Transsibérien*
1974	exhibits her major works at the Grenoble Museum
1975	named officer of the Légion d'Honneur
	Executes a poster for UNESCO on the occasion of International Women's Year
	Retrospective at the International Cultural Centre in Antwerp
	Exhibition at Galerie Sapone in Nice
	Exhibition 'Hommage à Sonia Delaunay' at the Musée National d'art moderne, Paris
	Exhibitions in Cologne, Naples and Tokyo

1977   publication by Jacques Damase of Tzara's *Le Coeur à gaz* illustrated with 10 lithographs by Sonia Delaunay
Participates in the exhibition 'Tendencies of the 1920s' organized by the Council of Europe in Berlin
Reproduction of certain textiles created in 1925 in connection with an exhibition at Artcurial, Paris
Presentation to the Bibliothèque nationale of the graphic works of Robert and Sonia Delaunay with a catalogue raisonné

1978–79   exhibition of drawings at Artcurial
Executes the poster for Jacques Damases's 30 years as publisher at the Centre Pompidou, Paris
Retrospective exhibitions in the USA and in Japan
Dies on 5 December 1979

Books with Illustrations by Sonia Delaunay

Album avec 6 gravures, Paris 1962

Cendrars, Blaise *La Prose du Transsibérien et de la Petite Jehanne de France*, Paris 1913

Damase Jacques *Alphabet*, Paris 1969 (Italian and English language editions published in Milan and New York 1972)

Damase, Jacques *Rhythmes et Couleurs* (pochoirs), Paris 1966

Damase, Jacques *Robes Poèmes*, Paris 1969

10 Origines (album of 10 original lithographs by Arp, Bill, Delaunay, Domela, Kandinsky, Lohse, Luppi, Magnelli, Taeuber-Arp and Vantongerloo), Zurich 1942

Rimbaud, Arthur *Les Illuminations* (pochoirs), Paris 1973

Tzara, Tristan *Le Coeur à gaz* (costumes by Sonia Delaunay), Paris 1977 (reprint of costume projects of 1923)

Tzara, Tristan *Juste présent*, Milan 1961

Writings of Sonia Delaunay

'L'Art de la Devanture', *Présentations*, 1934

'Les Artistes et l'avenir de la mode', *Revue de Jacques Heim*, No. 3, September 1932

'Collages de Sonia et Robert Delaunay', *XXe Siècle*, No. 6, January 1956, pp. 19–21

'Compositions, couleurs, idées', Paris 1930

L'Influence de la peinture sur l'art vestimentaire, Sorbonne conference 27 January 1927

'Lettre à un client', in catalogue of the Sonia Delaunay exhibition at the Städtliches Kunsthaus, Bielefeld 1958

Nous irons jusqu'au soleil, Paris 1978

'Robert et Sonia Delaunay, Art et mouvement, la Couleur dansée', *Art d'aujourd'hui, art et architecture*, Vol 3, No. 17, Boulogne-sur-Seine 1958

'Tissus et tapis', *L'Art international d'aujourd'hui*, No. 15, Paris 1929 (Editions d'Art Charles Moreau)

Untitled text for an album of lithographs, Milan 1966

Books about Sonia Delaunay

Anscombe, Isabelle *A Woman's Touch: Women in Design from 1960 to the Present Day*, London/New York 1985

Atelier simultané di Sonia Delaunay 1923–1934, Milan 1984

Cohen, Arthur A. *Sonia Delaunay*, New York 1975

Damase, Jacques (ed.) *Sonia Delaunay. Robes et gouaches simultanés, 1925. L'Art et le corps. Rhythmes-Couleurs en mouvement*, Brussels 1974

Damase, Jacques *L'Hommage à Sonia Delaunay*, Paris-Brussels 1976

Damase, Jacques *Sonia Delaunay, Rhythmes et Couleurs*, Paris 1971 (English language ed., London/New York 1972)

Damase, Jacques *Sonia Delaunay, dessins noirs et blancs*, Paris 1978

Damase, Jacques and Mustelier, Edouard *Sonia Delaunay*, Paris 1971

Ferreira, Paulo *Correspondance de quatre artistes portugais, Almada-Negreiros, José Pacheco, Souza-Cardoso, Eduardo Vianna, avec Robert et Sonia Delaunay*, Paris 1972

Hoog, Michel *Robert et Sonia Delaunay*, Paris 1967

Lhote, André *Sonia Delaunay; Ses peintures, ses objets, ses tissus simultanées, ses modes*, Paris 1925

Sonia Delaunay, La Terra impareggiabile, Milan 1971

Vreeland, Diana *Sonia Delaunay, Art in Fashion*, New York 1986

Selected Articles about Sonia Delaunay

Abadie, Daniel, 'Les Inventions simultaneés de Sonia Delaunay ou l'heure avant l'heure', *XXe Siècle*, Vol. XXXVIII, No. 46, (Paris) September 1976, pp. 20–27

'Agam, Arman, Cruz-Diaz, S. Delaunay, Vasarely. Réalités leur confie cinq voitures', *Connaissance des arts*, No. 188, (Paris) October 1966, pp. 85–86

Applegate, J., 'Paris, Sonia Delaunay, Galerie La Demeure', *Art International*, Vol. XIV, No. 3, (Lugano) May 1970, p. 74

'Aquarellen und Gouachen von 1912 bis 1958', Galerie Suzanne Bollag, Zürich, *Werk*, Vol. XLVI, No. 9, (Winterthur) September 1959, p. 194

Barber, Alice, 'Sonia Delaunay', *Craft Horizons*, Vol. XXXIII, No. 6, (New York), December 1973, pp. 32–39

Baron, Jeanine, 'Sonia Delaunay et ses amis Maiakovsky et Kandinsky', *La Croix*, (Brussels) 30 November 1975

Belloli, Carlo, 'I Delaunay e la grafica', *Pagina*, No. 2, (Milan) June 1963, pp. 4–22

Benoist, Luc, 'Les Tissus de Sonia Delaunay', *Art et décoration*, Vol. I, (Paris) March 1926, pp. 142–45

Berger, M. and Jelensky, K.A., 'La Peinture russe moderne', *Preuves*, No. III, (Paris) May 1960

Bousset, Maiten 'Les Lithographies de Sonia Delaunay', *XXe Siècle*, Vol. XXXI, No. 32, (Paris) June 1969, pp. 13–14

Cabanne, Pierre, 'Sonia Delaunay est depuis 50 ans à l'avant-garde', *Arts*, No. 951, (Paris) 26 February–3 November 1964, p. 8

'Le Cabinet des dessins de Sonia Delaunay', *Journal Artcurial*, No. 11, (Paris) October 1978, pp. 1–5

'Le Cabinet des dessins de Sonia Delaunay, Artcurial, Paris', *L'Oeil*, No. 280, (Paris) November 1978, p. 66

Chatwin, Bruce, 'Surviving in Style', *The New York Times Magazine*, 4 March 1973, pp. 42–54

'Cinq voitures de série personalisés par cinq artistes contemporains. Une expérience louée par Réalités au profit de la Fondation pour la recherche médicale française', *Réalités*, (Paris) October 1967, pp. 82–87

Clay, Jean, 'Sonia Delaunay', *Le Arti*, Vol. XXIV, No. 1, (Milan) January 1974, pp. 12–48

Clay, Jean, 'The Golden Years of Visual Jazz: Sonia Delaunay, Life and Times', *Réalités* (English edition), Paris 1965, pp. 42–47

Cohen, Arthur A., 'The Delaunays, Apollinaire and Cendrars', in *Critiques 1971--1972*, The Cooper Union School of Art and Architecture, New York, Autumn 1972, pp. 1–16

Craven, Arthur, 'L'Exposition des Indépendants', *Maintenant* (special issue), (Paris) May-April 1914, pp. 1–17

Crevel, René, 'Visite à Sonia Delaunay', *La Voz de Guipuzcoa*, Bilbao 1920

Damase, Jacques, 'Sonia Delaunay, Great Lady of Abstract Art', *Art: the Journal of the Professional Arts*, UNESCO Paris, No. 64–65, 1971–1972, pp. 26–31

Damase, Jacques, 'Sonia Delaunay, 60 ans de recherches et d'innovations', *XXe Siècle*, Vol. XXIX, No. 29, (Paris) December 1967, pp. 108–12

Damase, Jacques, 'Un demi-siècle d'avant-garde', *Connaissance des arts*, No. 308 (Paris) 1977, pp. 80–85

d'Aubarède, G., 'Sonia Delaunay évoque des souvenirs', *Le Jardin des arts*, (Paris) January 1963, pp. 2–9

Degand, Léon, 'Sonia Delaunay et l'exaltation chromatique', *XXe Siècle*, (Paris) June 1956, pp. 82–85

Delteil, Joseph, 'La Mode qui vient à Mme Sonia Delaunay', *Europe Almanach*, (Potsdam) 1925, pp. 207–10

De Torre, Guillermo, 'El Arte decorativo de Sonia Delaunay', *Alfar*, No. 35, (Montevideo) December 1923

Dorival, Bernard, 'Les Oeuvres récentes de Sonia Delaunay', *XXe Siècle*, Vol. XXXIII, (Paris) June 1971, pp. 42–50

Dorival, Bernard, 'Robert et Sonia Delaunay', *Coloquio*, No. 35, (Lisbon) 1965, pp. 8–13

Dormoy, Marie, 'Les Tissus de Sonia Delaunay', *L'Amour de l'art*, Vol. VIII, (Paris) March 1927, pp. 97–98

Francastel, Pierre, 'Les Delaunay', *XXe Siècle*, Vol. XXII, No. 15, (Paris) December 1960, pp. 64–73

Georg, Charles, 'Les Marchés au Minho de Sohia Delaunay', *Bulletin du Musée d'Art et d'Histoire de Genève*, Vol. XIII, (Geneva) 1965, pp. 203–13

Gilioli, Emile, 'Les Tapis de Sonia Delaunay', *XXe Siècle*, Vol. XXXII, No. 34, (Paris) June 1970, pp. 13–17

Gindertael, Michel, 'Oeuvres récentes de Sonia Delaunay', *XXe Siècle*, Vol. XXX, No. 31, (Paris) December 1968, pp. 57–64

Gindertael, R.V., 'Pour aider à mieux comprendre le passage de la ligne', *Art d'aujourd'hui*, 3rd series, No. 6 (Boulogne-sur-Seine) August 1952, pp. 18–22

Gindertael, R.V., 'Robert Delaunay-Sonia Delaunay', *Art d'aujourd'hui*, 3rd series, No. 6, (Boulogne-sur-Seine) August 1952, pp. 20–21

Gindertael, R.V., 'Sonia Delaunay et la poésie pure des couleurs', *XXe Siècle*, Vol. XXV, No. 21, (Paris) May 1963, pp. 43–47

Giroud, Françoise, 'Ahead of Her Time in Tune with Ours', *The New York Times Magazine*, – July 1978, pp. 54–59

Goll, Claire, 'Simultanische Kleider', *Bilder Kurier*, (Berlin) April 1924

Gomez de la Serna, Ramon, 'Los Trajes Poematicos', *Le Voz de Guipuzcoa*, (Bilbao) 1922

Habasque, Guy, 'L'Oeuvre de Robert et Sonia Delaunay', *Vie des Arts*, No. 4, (Montreal) winter 1965–66

Hoog, Michel, 'Les Tissus de Sonia Delaunay au Musée des tissus', *Bulletin des musées et monuments lyonnais*, Lyons 1968, pp. 85–93

Hoog, Michel, 'Oeuvres récents de Sonia Delaunay', *Cimaise*, Vol. XV, No. 88–89, (Paris) October 1968, pp. 52–63

Hoog, Michel, 'Quelques précurseurs de l'art d'aujourd'hui', *Revue de Louvre*, Vol. XVI, No. 3, (Paris) May-June 1966, pp. 165–72

Jung-Clemenceau, Thérèse, 'La Boutique simultanée', *Les Arts plastiques*, No. 2, (Paris) 1925

Lansner, Fay, 'Arthur Cohen on Sonia Delaunay', *The Feminist Art Journal*, Vol. 5, No. 4, (New York) winter 1976–1977, pp. 5–10

Lassaigne, Jacques, 'Gouaches de Sonia Delaunay', *XXe Siècle*, Vol. XXIV, No. 19, (Paris) June 1962, pp. 18–19

Lassaigne, Jacques, 'Robert et Sonia Delaunay', *Pensées françaises*, No.

5, (Paris) May 1960, pp. 62–66

Lévèque, Jean-Jacques, 'Le Siècle de Sonia Delaunay', *Les Nouvelles Littéraires*, 24 November 1975

Lévèque, Jean-Jacques, 'Sonia Delaunay al Naviglio, Venezia', *Le Arti*, Vol. XIX, No. 7–8, (Milan) August 1969, pp. 14–16

Marter, Joan M., 'Three Women Artists Married to Early Modernists, Sonia Delaunay-Terk, Sophie Taeuber-Arp and Marguerite Thompson-Zorach', *Arts Magazine*, Vol. LIV, No. 1, (New York) September 1979, pp. 89–95

Mazars, Pierre, 'L'Art a suivi Sonia Delaunay dans la rue', *Le Figaro*, Paris, 25 November 1975

Mellow, James, 'When Her Husband Died She Came into Her Own', *The New York Times*, 27 January 1974

Mertens, Phil, 'Het Overzicht en de Plaats van de Vlaamse Kunst in het Europa van de Jaren Twintig', *Bulletin du Musée Royal des Beaux-Arts de Belgique*, Vol. XIII, (Brussels) 1964, pp. 67–82

Metkin, Gunter, 'The Delaunay's [sic] Theatre', *Art and the Stage in the Twentieth Century: Painters and Sculptors Work for the Theater* (ed. Henning Rischbieter), Greenwich, Conn., 1969, pp. 105–06

Michel, Jacques, 'Sonia Delaunay at Ninety', *The Guardian*, London, 21 December 1975

Ornella, Barbara, 'L'Hommage de Lisbonne à Robert et Sonia Delaunay', *XXe Siècle*, Vol. XXXIV, No. 39, (Paris) December 1972, pp. 101–12

Ornella, Barbara, 'Portugal na vida e na obra de Sonia Delaunay (1915–1916)', *Coloquio*, Vol. XIV, No. 8, (Lisbon) July 1972, pp. 53–63

Peppiati, Michael, 'Sonia Delaunay', *Art International*, Vol. XVII, No. 10, (Lugano) December 1973, pp. 18, 19, 35

Peppiati, Michael, 'Sonia Delaunay, a Life in Color', *Art News*, Vol. LXXIV, No. 3, (New York) March 1975, pp. 88–91

Petzet, Heinrich, 'Robert und Sonia Delaunay in der Basler Galerie d'Art moderne', *Weltkunst*, Vol. XXXII, No. 16, (Berlin) 1961, p. 7

Ragon, Michel, 'Les Delaunay, une couple fou de couleurs', in *Les Vies des grands peintres*, Paris 1962

Ragon, Michel, 'Sonia Delaunay a fait entrer le Cubisme dans la mode et dans la vie', *Arts*, No. 866, (Paris) April-May 1962, p. 11

Rickey, Carrie, 'Sonia Delaunay: Theater of Color', *Art in America*, No. 68, (New York) May 1980, pp. 90–101

Seuphor, Michel, 'L'Orphisme', *Art d'aujourd'hui*, 1st series, Nos. 7–8, (Bologne-sur-Seine) March 1950, pp. 25–26

'Sonia Delaunay', *Journal Artcurial*, No. 7–8, (Paris) December 1977, pp. 1–5

'Sonia Delaunay', *Spare Rib*, No. 18, (London) December 1973, p. 30

'Sonia Delaunay, fifty years not gone by', *Domus*, No. 555, (Milan) January 1976, pp. 52–53

'Sonia Delaunay Tapestries', *Artweek*, Vol. V, No. 34, (Oakland) 1974, p. 5

Sternberg, E., 'Sonia Delaunay-Terk', *Kunstwerk*, Vol. XV, No. 4, (Baden-Baden) October 1961, pp. 22–23

Strauss, M., 'Exhibition at Brook Street Gallery', *Burlington Magazine*, Vol. CIII, No. 699, (London) June 1961, pp. 288–91

'Tous les arts de la danse', *Connaissance des arts*, No. 202, (Paris), December 1968, pp. 29–31

Van Loon, H., 'Waar Kunst en Mode Elkaar Ontmoeten', *Maandblad voor Beeldende Kunsten*, Vol. VI, (Amsterdam) September 1929, pp. 276–81

Vieira, José Geraldo, 'Affinidades Analogies e Coincidéncias', *Habitat*, Vol. VI, No. 32, (Sao Paulo) 1956, pp. 7–11

Vincent, Madeleine, 'Trois tableaux de Robert and Sonia Delaunay', *Bulletin des musées et monuments lyonnais*, Vol. III, No. 1, (Lyons) 1962, pp. 1–8

Wadia, Bettina, 'Sonia Delaunay at Gimpel Fils', *Art Review*, Vol. XVIII, No. 2, (London) February 1966, p. 25

Wallen, Burr, 'Sonia Delaunay and Pochoir', *Arts Magazine*, Vol. LIV, No. 1, (New York) September 1979, pp. 96–102

Weelen, Guy, 'Los Delaunay en España y Portugal', *Goya*, No. 48, (Madrid) May-June 1962, pp. 420–29

Weelen, Guy, 'Robes simultanées, Sonia Delaunay s'amusa longtemps à habiller les femmes', *L'Oeil*, No. 60, (Paris) December 1959, pp. 78–85

Weelen, Guy, 'Sonia Delaunay en Allemagne', *XXe Siècle*, Vol. XXI, No. 12, (Paris) May-June 1959, pp. 12–13

Wescher, Herta, 'Eaux vives et Sources taries', *Cimaise*, series V, No. 3, (Paris) January-Feburary 1958, pp. 23–31

Wierer, M., 'Sonia Delaunay, Jongleur der Farbe', *Alte und moderne Kunst*, Vol. XXI, No. 145, (Vienna) 1976, pp. 20–25

Wright, Barbara, 'Sonia Delaunay', *Art Review*, Vol. XXVI, No. 14, (London) 1974, p. 363

Exhibition catalogues

Damase, Jacques *Robert et Sonia Delaunay*, Lisbon (Gulbenkian Foundation) 1982

Damase, Jacques *Robert et Sonia Delaunay*, Madrid (Fondation March) 1982

Ferreira, Paulo *Sonia et Robert Delaunay au Portugal et leurs amis E. Vianna, A. Souza-Cardoso, Pacheco Almada-Negreiros, à la Fondation Gulbenkian à Lisbonne*, 1972

Hoog, Michel *Robert Delaunay à l'Orangerie des Tuileries*, Paris 1976

Hoog, Michel and Dorival, Bernard *Retrospective Sonia Delaunay au Musée national d'art moderne*, Paris 1967

Robert et Sonia Delaunay 1885–1985, Paris (Musée d'art moderne de la ville de Paris) 1985

Six artistes à Grasse 1940–1943, Grasse (Société du Musée Fragonard, Musée régional d'art et d'histoire) 1967

Sonia et Robert Delaunay, Paris (Bibliothèque Nationale) 1977

Tuck, Robert T. *Sonia Delaunay 1886–1979*, Buffalo 1980

Index